Carol Peterson

From Then

'til Now

Nearly 100 Years

Trafford Publishing
Victoria, British Columbia
CANADA

From Then...'til Now
© Copyright 2004, Carol Peterson.
All rights reserved.

Pictures on Cover:
Upper Left: 1917. Mama Helen, with my oldest sister Arlene.
Upper Right: 1937. Carol, cultivating young corn.
Middle Left: 1945. Carol in Army uniform, while in
Germany in World War II.
Middle Right: 1975. Carol during the booming days of
the pallet business.
Lower Left: 1970. Back L-R: Mike, Arlen, Kathy, Dwight,
Patty. Front L-R: Wendy, Irene holding
Tammy, Carol, Susan holding Wanda.
Lower Right: 2004. Irene and Carol.

TRAFFORD

No part of this publication may be reproduced, stored in a retrieval system, or transmitted, in any form or by any means, electronic, mechanical, photocopying, recording, or otherwise, without the written prior permission of the author.

Note for Librarians: a cataloguing record for this book that includes Dewey Decimal Classification and US Library of Congress numbers is available from the National Library of Canada. The complete cataloguing record can be obtained from the National Library's online database at:
www.nlc-bnc.ca/amicus/index-e.html
ISBN 1-4120-4622-x

Offices in Canada, USA, Ireland, UK and Spain
This book was published *on-demand* in cooperation with Trafford Publishing. On-demand publishing is a unique process and service of making a book available for retail sale to the public taking advantage of on-demand manufacturing and Internet marketing. On-demand publishing includes promotions, retail sales, manufacturing, order fulfilment, accounting and collecting
royalties on behalf of the author.

Book sales in Europe:
Trafford Publishing (UK) Ltd., Enterprise House, Wistaston Road Business Centre, Wistaston Road, Crewe CW2 7RP UNITED KINGDOM
phone 01270 251 396 (local rate 0845 230 9601)
facsimile 01270 254 983; info.uk@trafford.com

Book sales for North America and international:
Trafford Publishing, 6E–2333 Government St.,
Victoria, BC V8T 4P4 CANADA
phone 250 383 6864 (toll-free 1 888 232 4444)
fax 250 383 6804; email to bookstore@trafford.com

www.trafford.com/robots/04-2430.html

10 9 8 7 6 5 4 3 2

Acknowledgments

There are two or three people that I must give credit to for making this book possible.

No. 1: my wife, Irene, who has listened to me and helped me in my thinking. She took my scribbled writing and typed it on the computer, and also helped to find pictures, etc.

No. 2: Janice (Baker) Lepinski. Janice is my sister Dorothy's daughter. Dorothy passed away a few years ago. Janice is really in partnership with Irene and me on this project. She has put it all on the computer and organized the pictures in the proper places. Janice has been great and has done a wonderful job. She has been patient with me when I decided to change something she had already done, meaning she needed to do it over.

No. 3: Jerry Lepinski, Janice's husband. Jerry has served as advisor and helper in getting some special pictures, and he has also been a "go-between" for us, driving back and forth from Minneapolis, Minnesota to Frederic, Wisconsin several times.

P.S.: All my life I have wondered why my parents put my name on my birth certificate spelled like a girl. It has been somewhat of a problem all my life. I have threatened to change the spelling, but never did. I still get phone calls asking for Carol, and when I say "That's me," the person on the other end is surprised, as they were expecting to talk to a woman.

Irene Peterson

Janice and Jerry Lepinski. Janice is the daughter of the author's sister, Dorothy Baker.

Table of Contents

Preface i
Before My Time ii
Chapter One: Family: Early Days 1
Chapter Two: Spirit Lake School + ...11
Chapter Three: Steam Power, Early Cars, Etc. 19
Chapter Four: The Thirties 31
Chapter Five: Steam, Gas and Diesel 39
Chapter Six: Rumors of War and Army Days 49
Chapter Seven: Coming Home and Getting Started 63
Chapter Eight: Married Life 71
Chapter Nine: Losing My Finger + ...85
Chapter Ten: Buying Birchwood Beach 89
Chapter Eleven: Marrying Irene 95
Chapter Twelve: Family Life and Daddy's Death 103
Chapter Thirteen: Sawmill, Pallet Business + ...109
Chapter Fourteen: Business and Finances 115
Chapter Fifteen: Campground Church Services + ...123
Chapter Sixteen: Looking Back 125
Chapter Seventeen: Kids Growing Up 131
Chapter Eighteen: Sawmill Fire + ...135
Chapter Nineteen: Selling to Dwight and Nancy 143
Chapter Twenty: Irene's Heart Attack 149
Chapter Twenty-One: Irene's Own Words 153
Chapter Twenty-Two: Our New House 157
Chapter Twenty-Three: Politics 161
Chapter Twenty-Four: Reminiscing 165

Pictures 168

Preface

This book is dedication and reason for attempting to write a book of changes and progress made in the last 100 years in the world and in our country; this as seen through my 80 plus years of living, mostly in beautiful, northwest Wisconsin.

I have felt for many years that there have perhaps never been a 75 to 100 years that have seen so much progress and change, both for good and bad. Life has always been mixed with both good times and bad times, and so it will until the Lord returns. But this type of good and bad is not what I am writing about. In the horse and buggy era and early years of the car, there were a lot of hard times: poverty, sickness, and epidemics, but by and large, the moral fiber of most people was much better than now.

There are many things to blame, but the sad part of this is that I believe the Christians are the most to blame for not getting involved. The scapegoat idea: it's all in the Lord's hands, we don't have to worry or do anything. In the meantime, much has happened because of the ACLU, our court system, the pressure of the entertainment world and the Democratic party, and too many Republicans voting wrong. It is already illegal for the kids to pray in school or even take their Bible to school. They are trying to get "In God We Trust" off our money and take for God and Country out of the Pledge of Allegiance.

However, I feel there is a trend now of thinking seriously about God and morals and hard work, and there will have to be if this world is going to last. So I am dedicating this to my nine children, grandchildren and great grandchildren and anyone who reads it that it will help them see what a change has taken place in the 1900's and that it might help them on the road of life, plus hopefully bring some enjoyment.

Following is a memory that has stuck in my mind ever since hearing my Dad or uncle tell it when I was a kid, perhaps eight  or ten years old. My uncle had a beautiful garden, and one day he was working in it when the Circuit Riding Preacher (which I almost remember from those days) came by and was visiting with and witnessing to my uncle. He said "This sure is a beautiful garden that you and the Lord have here." My uncle's response was "Yeah, but you should have seen it when the Lord had it by Himself."

i

Before My Time: 1880's to 1920's

This writing is in August, 2004, as we are hopefully soon going to print. In looking at my sister Arlene (Peterson) Lee's book of 1987, I thought I would like to give a tribute to my ancestors who left Sweden, selling everything to be able to afford to come to the United States, to hopefully start a new life for themselves and their loved ones in a new land.

The hardships they went through are unbelievable, but once they decided to take their families and go to a new land, there was no backing out; they just had to make the best of it. This was not only the story for the Swedes, but also for the people of many of the countries of Europe. I don't know much of what the situation was in Europe at the time, but coming to the United States must have looked to them as the thing to do. In a lot of cases, it had to do with religion and religious freedom. They must have been the most hard-working, adventurous people, and I believe this is really the root of what made the United States the great country that it is.

The ads that follow are a little before my time, but a lot of these, (stationary engine, etc.) were still in use in the 1920's and 1930's, so I have memories of them. I don't recall this Stover in our area. We had a 3 HP International Fairbank Morse and others, but basically they all looked somewhat the same. The big, heavy flywheels were weighted to help them have more power. In the 1920's and 1930's, electricity started coming in, so they were no longer needed. Electric power was taking over.

Back L-R: Great-Grandpa Okerstrom, Grandma Olivia, Augusta, Albert (Dad). Front L-R: Charley, Freda, Hilive.

Ads for machinery in a magazine from 1923.

Stover Model CT 1½ hp Engine, built in 1928.

Stover engines of 1920 could be purchased in 3 to 12 hp sizes in this model.

3 & 6 H.P. Type "K" Engines Are NOW Ready

Inspired by the success of our 1½ H. P. Type "K" Engine—famous as "The Engine With 16 Distinctive Features"—we have just put into quantity production two more Stover Type "K" Engines—one of 3 H. P. and the other a 6 H. P. Size.

Some Outstanding Features

They possess all the qualities that made the the 1½ H. P. popular—throttling governor for kerosene or gasoline, hit and miss for gasoline only, water-cooled cylinder head, removable die-cast bearings, shims for taking up wear, etc.

Write for FREE Booklet

Get our FREE Engine Booklet. Dealers everywhere are seeking representation for our engine line, thereby entrenching themselves as the leaders in their territory. Those who write us *immediately* may be able to secure dealerships in their vicinity.

Stover Manufacturing and Engine Co.

Also makers of *Stover Samson Windmills, Ensilage Cutters, Comminuters, Pump Jacks, Working Heads, Wood Saw Frames, Hot Galvanized Steel Fence Posts, Itclued Electric Light Plants and Hardware Specialties.*

1611 Lake St.   FREEPORT, ILL.

1992 Featured Engine Stovers Good Engines

A Stover pin of 1922.

A Stover engine ad which appeared in a 1923 issue of Farm Magazine.

With a gasoline-powered machine, the farmer's wife had leisure time on washday. (USDA)

In its first application to farming, the gasoline engine was used almost entirely to pump water for livestock, often replacing the windmill already in operation. Subsequently, it was called upon to pump water into the house for domestic use. There it became the women folks' best helper, turning the washing machine, cream separator, churn, and a dynamo for lighting the home and premises. Soon it was sawing firewood, grinding feed, and performing a dozen other chores around the farmstead. Thus, step by step, the range of usefulness and influence of the gasoline engine broadened.

The acquisition of that first gas engine was an occasion to be long remembered, as one farmer related in the **Gas Review** in 1909:

> . . . so taking all points into consideration I ordered a new engine. When it came and I got it home, all I had to do was hitch on the battery, put in some gasoline, fill the reservoir, or jacket, with water, turn the wheel and away it went. The whole family and half of the neighborhood were in attendance. I realized that there would be many sacrifices before it was paid for, but the feeling of having an engine of my own balanced up any thought of sacrifice I might be called upon to make.

Note the "Business Course free" ad.

THE NORTH DAKOTA FARMER

Business Course Free

Do you want a business course in one of the best Business colleges in the Northwest?

Here is Your Chance

We want one ambitious young man in each county to represent the North Dakota Farmer. We are willing to pay liberally for a little work. You can easily obtain the required number of subscribers at the Farmers' Institute held in your county.

Here is the Plan

For only 100 New Subscriptions at 50 cents a year we will furnish free three months' tuition, worth $25, in one of our best Business Colleges, and besides we will pay a cash commission of $10 to help expenses.

Write Now

If you are interested, as we shall make this arrangement with but one representative in each county of the state.

E. F. LADD & CO., Lisbon

To MILWAUKEE CHICAGO the EAST and SOUTH use the

Wisconsin Central

Comfortable, solid wide vestibuled trains, leaving Minneapolis and St. Paul every morning and evening at convenient hours, equipped with Pullman Sleepers, Free Reclining Chair Cars and modern coaches. Meals in dining and cafe cars served a la carte. For tickets and further information apply to nearest ticket agent or write,

JAS. C. POND, General Pass. Agt.,
MILWAUKEE, WIS.

The Stover Engine

A BOY CAN RUN IT

For Simplicity, Reliability, Finish, Low Price, and, above all, Durability, the Stover is unexcelled.
Before handling the engine we thoroughly tested the engine for years.
Write for bed-rock prices

LISBON WOOD AND IRON WORKS.

50 YEARS' EXPERIENCE
PATENTS
TRADE MARKS
DESIGNS
COPYRIGHTS &c.
Anyone sending a sketch and description may quickly ascertain our opinion free whether an invention is probably patentable. Communications strictly confidential. HANDBOOK on Patents sent free. Oldest agency for securing patents.
Patents taken through Munn & Co. receive special notice, without charge, in the

Scientific American.

A handsomely illustrated weekly. Largest circulation of any scientific journal. Terms, $3 a year; four months, $1. Sold by all newsdealers.
MUNN & Co. 361 Broadway, New York
Branch Office, 625 F St., Washington, D. C.

STONES MUSIC HOUSE
EVERYTHING KNOWN IN MUSIC
FARGO — N. DAKOTA

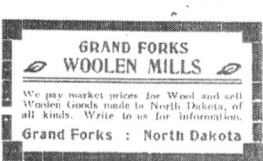

GRAND FORKS
WOOLEN MILLS
We pay market prices for Wool and sell Woolen Goods made in North Dakota, of all kinds. Write to us for information.
Grand Forks : North Dakota

"The North Dakota Farmer," a magazine published at Lisbon, N.D., contained this Stover engine ad in No. 4, Vol. 7 issue of November 1905.

WMSTR-302

Cut-out picture of a modern 1900's house, before the advent of convenient electricity.

Engines were used to drive an overhead power take-off line shaft which was powered by a 4 inch wide belt. Various appliances were then connected to the line shaft with additional 4 inch wide belts.

Some of the equipment visible in this picture (left-right) are a planer for surfacing lumber, the motor for driving the line shaft, a fan for circulation, a creamer, and a washing machine.

This overhead power take-off line shaft system was used so that several appliances could be run off of one engine, unlike today, where every appliance has its own electrical motor, and you simply plug them in to the electrical outlet. These wide belts were removed from appliances you didn't want running. These belts were also unguarded and dangerous. Many accidents and injuries were caused by the belts grabbing appendages and pulling them through the drive wheels.

These systems were not common, they were used by the more wealthy who could afford it.

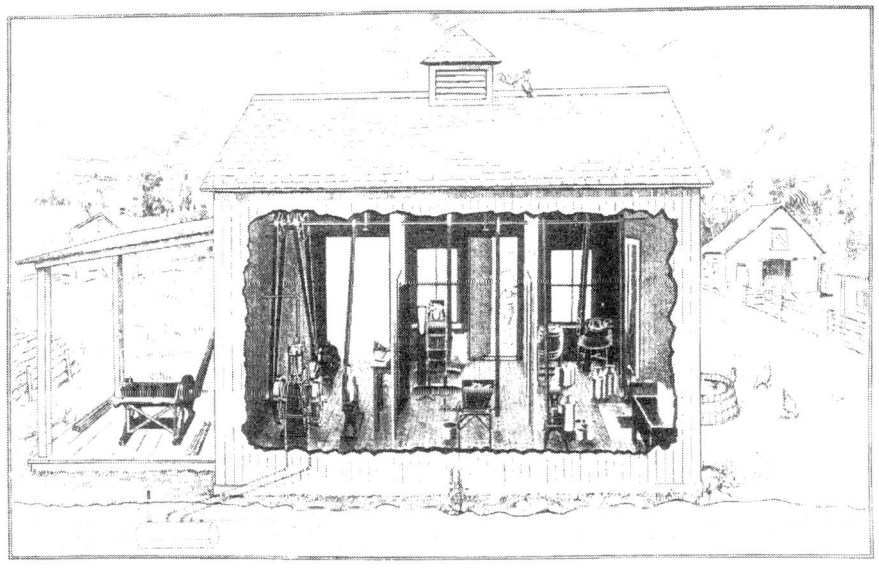

Engines from late 1800's through the 1930's.

The style of gas engine selected was determined by the location and the nature of the work to be performed. Operating a farm powerhouse, for instance, required the use of a stationary engine. This example, manufactured by the Stover Engine Company, was available in sizes ranging from 4- to 12-horsepower.

Chapter One: Family: Early Days

It was the winter of 1922-1923; I was never told and too young to remember, but if it was a typical northwest winter, it was most likely cold and snowy. There was the excitement of Christmas coming, but in the Peterson house there was extra excitement because they were expecting a new arrival. The three girls: Arlene about 6, Bernice about 4, and Loretta about 2, along with Mom and Dad, were excited because Mom was going to have a baby.

In those days, most babies were born at home, which was the case. They had seen Dr. Swanson, who lived about four miles away at 4 Corners and he predicted it would come real close to Christmas. So they had the name Carol picked out, I guess expecting a girl; but it didn't come and didn't come until January 29th, 1923. A neighbor lady (Mrs. Turner), assisted by my Dad, brought me into this world. I was told by Mrs. Turner's daughter that her mother did the honors for about 35 babies around the area at that time. I can just imagine the smile on my Dad's face to find out it was a boy after three girls. But they still stuck with the name Carol and still spelled it Carol just like a girl's name. That has been somewhat of a problem all my life, but I never changed it.

I don't think I recall very much until maybe 1925, when my next sister, Dorothy, was born. A few years later, in 1927, our family got electricity (ours was one of the first in our area to have that luxury), but the kerosene lamps and lanterns were kept ready to go if the electricity failed, as well as for rooms or outer buildings that weren't wired.

About 1928.
Back L-R: Arlene, Loretta, Bernice.
Front L-R: Carol, Dorothy.

My Dad was, in my mind to this day, a Genius to be able to take discarded machines - or whatever - and create something to make life easier, and yet not spend money to do it. Money was very scarce and with a big family you had to figure out a way to get along. This was not long after the end of World War I, and things were pretty tough, I guess. But somehow we children were unaware of being poor and I think we were as happy and content as any children could be, rich or poor. We were taught the love of God and our parents and extended family of relatives and neighbors. Sunday School and Church were very much a part of our life, even though Dad had had some problems in church, so he would seldom go; but he made sure we were there. He would bring us in the 1917 Model T Ford, which was our car, or with the horses and sled if the snow was too deep. Again it seemed that we were more blessed than many of our neighbors who didn't have cars.

Another luxury that we had (or Dad managed to get) was a battery radio. He would sit in the evenings with his earphones on and listen to what was on. One of the first really exciting things I remember was when Charles Lindbergh flew across the ocean. I was only 4 years old, but I remember how exciting it was, I think maybe because Daddy was so excited about it. That was really something.

Another vivid memory I have is of Memorial Day. Since our home was only about a mile away, we would not go to the graveyard, but be outside when they would shoot over the graves and then Daddy would explain about World War I and what it meant. My Dad was not a veteran, but had uncles and neighbors who were. It seemed to me that there was a great feeling of loyalty and love of country that made for happy, satisfied people.

About 1910. Albert (Dad), Grandpa Okerstrom

Barn built by Albert (Dad) in 1912.

We lived on 160 acres that was homesteaded by Grandpa (my Dad's father). Grandpa was killed in 1896 in a sawmill accident. Daddy was only 8 years old and had to be the man of the place, but his Grandpa on his mother's side lived close by, so was a big help. They kept struggling along until Dad decided to go west and worked on the railroad for a couple of years. However, the love of home and the fact that most of his brothers and sisters had left for Canada, meant his mother needed help. So he came home to help her farm.

In about 1910 the original barn burned, and in 1912 Daddy built a new barn 36 ft. by 80 ft., which was big for a barn at that time. It was cement block to the haymow and he made all the blocks by hand. In November 1912, his mother died, he struggled along alone but it wasn't going well, so in March of 1914 he had an auction and sold out, but kept the farm.

On July 16th, 1914 Daddy married my mother, Ida Helen Larson. They had a quite extensive honeymoon for those days. Following is an excerpt from Mom's diary of the trip.

Albert and Ida Helen, 1914

Started July 17th, at 2:45 PM. At Minneapolis same evening. July 18th spent afternoon seeing Barney Oldfield and Lincoln Beachy racing; auto and aeroplane. Left Minneapolis at 6:25 PM. At Chicago 7:50 AM. July 19th, spent the day in beautiful Lincoln Park. Also had our first ride on Lake Michigan. Got safely to our hotel very, very tired. July 20th went to the observation tower at Boston store. Went through the Art Institute, Academy of Sciences, and had an auto ride around the park. July 21st, left at 9:30 AM on Str. City of Benton Harbor. Arrived at St. Joe at 1:46 PM. Took in the sights until 5:00 PM when we left on the same boat for Chicago. Had a very nice trip. July 22nd, in the park and around town. July 23rd, left at 10:15 AM; arrived at Minneapolis at 10:45 PM hungry, tired, thirsty, and dirty. July 24th at Minneapolis. July 25th, left at 4:10 PM for Frederic. Safe at home at 10:45.

After the honeymoon, they moved to Minneapolis, where they lived until 1917. He worked in a streetcar factory. In those days the bodies were made mostly out of oak wood. It made a wood craftsman out of him that was second to none in my estimation. Then in 1917 my oldest sister Arlene was born and they moved back to the home farm and started farming again. We lived on that farm and where he lived until he was killed in a tractor accident in 1962.

The home farm by the 1930's had about 37 acres of cropland, and a small lake with good fishing. About one half of our farm was considered meadow and swampland, and a lot

The Home Farm.

of hilly wooded hardwood and pastureland. In my mind it was almost Heaven on Earth. We usually had 25 to 35 head of cattle, including an average of 16 milking cows, and a chicken house for about 200 laying hens. There was also a pig house and pen where we raised usually 10 to 25 hogs a year. We always kept our own bull to breed our cows. Back then there was no artificial breeding.

We were blessed with one thing on the home farm that most didn't have: gravel for the roads but also concrete gravel that was used in many buildings in the 1930's on WPA (Works Progress Administration) program. If it hadn't been for this I believe my Dad and stepmother would have lost the place in the 30's, but there was a lot of top soil to strip off first, so it really did make for a lot of work all done by horses and by hand. I have many memories of that gravel pit and working with Dad and Philip, our hired man. In today's world it would be unbearable and stupid hard work but to me it was fun and exciting.

Towards the north side of our home acreage (160 acres) there was a big elm tree five feet in diameter that was so tall it stood above all the other trees on the skyline when you looked from a hill on the road from Trade Lake. One day in the winter of 1929, Daddy was coming home from Trade Lake, and he couldn't see the tree above all the others. So when he got home, he walked back to see why, and he found the tree had been cut down.

The young men who did it had left their tracks in the snow, so Daddy followed them up to where they lived. They admitted they had cut it down because they thought there were raccoons in it. In those years, there was almost no work for teenagers, especially in the winter

Carol on big elm tree, 1929.

time, but there was a small bounty on coon skins. So they were hoping to make a few bucks. What a mistake! It was so big their cross-cut saw would hardly reach, so they had an almost impossible job sawing it down with the type of saw available at that time. They said it took them seven days to cut it down, and then no coons! What a bummer. They did wrong, but still in thinking back on it, I felt sorry for them. At the time I was only six years old, but I was already almost old enough to be trapping gophers, woodchucks, etc., to make some money. Those were poor years, but still fun years.

That tree meant everything to my Dad, and they did do wrong, so he went to the Burnett County Sheriff. It seems they made a deal; rather than being put in jail, they agreed to cut logs for creamery wood and firewood out of that tree, following my Dad's instructions. Knowing the kind of guy my Dad was, he probably brought them something to eat when he went out to see how they were doing. It took them seven weeks to cut all the logs, 3 foot creamery wood and stove wood out of that tree.

Elm tree being sawn into lumber.

All the farm work and in the gravel pit was done with horses until after I went in the Army in 1944, when Daddy bought his first tractor, a John Deere H, a one plow tractor.

Carol and horses about 1938.

All animals, especially the horses, were like part of the family. In all the years until I went into the Army for World War II, we only had eight horses in all. Most of the heavy work was done with three horse hitches, such as plowing, disking, pulling the corn or grain binder, as well as lighter work such as mowing hay, raking hay, and hauling hay. Seeding grain, etc. was done with a team of two horses. A lot of the cultivating was done with a one horse cultivator. The names of our horses were Ned, Nellie, and Bob and they were the work force long enough, so I got old enough to drive them a lot. I think Ned lived to be 32 years old and still full of spunk. Then there

About 1930.
Back L-R: Bernice, Arlene, Loretta.
Front L-R: Pearl, Dorothy, Carol.

was Nip and Tuck, a great team of bays. Then Bess was bought to replace Bob. She was the only horse I didn't like. She had a bad disposition. Then there was Babe and Buck, they were around for a long time after Dad bought his first tractor. So much for the place that was home to me and like I said before, almost Heaven on Earth to me.

To get back to my childhood, somehow I don't have much memory of when Dorothy was born; I guess I was just too young. I was two years old. But I do have memories of Pearl's birth. The family car was still the 1917 Model T. My mother was again expecting; it was in July. By that time she was going to have the baby in Frederic Hospital. I don't know the details, but it seems Daddy was in the field working with the horses and Mom went into labor. One of my sisters ran out to get him and they came rushing in and got Lizzy going, and rushed off for the hospital. I am sure Daddy had it going all of it's 45+ miles an hour, but it wasn't fast enough. So when they got to the hospital about 10 miles away, Pearl was already born, so they took baby and mother into the hospital separately, but it still turned out fine. They named her Pearl Elizabeth because the Model T Fords were nicknamed Tin Lizzies.

Another memory I have of that occasion was that when Mom and baby sister Pearl were ready to come home, I was allowed to go along. We got there about noon and Mama was just having dinner so we had to wait until she was done eating. Up to that time I had never heard of or had any tapioca pudding, which was what Mama had for dessert and she gave it to me. It was great and to this day whenever I have tapioca I think of that day.

In 1928, the first Model A Fords came out and believe it or not, even at 5 years old, I remember how exciting it was. I guess Daddy was always a Ford man, so we didn't see much of the other makes.

1929 must have been the year Daddy bought another Model T Ford (a 1926 two door) and retired the 1917. He never traded it in. It was in the machine shed for some years, then was moved down in the barnyard by a scrap iron pile for many years.

We played in it a lot. The 1926 had full doors and windows. The 1917 had open sides unless you put up the side curtains. I have one vivid recollection of a time Daddy took me along on one of his business trips in this 1917 Model T. I would have been 4 years old; we went way up on the other side of Webster to the Oakland store and then somewhere about 30 miles from home, and I really thought I had been on a long trip. The farthest I had ever been away from home, and to this day whenever we go by Oakland store I remember that day so long ago, and how far it was to ride in that open Ford.

1929 was one of the big years of my life. That was the year I started school, because you were supposed to be six years old to start and my birthday was in January. I ended up being over six and one half years old before I could start. In those days, at least in this area, there was no kindergarten, but with three older sisters I probably knew as much or more than kids who have gone to kindergarten these days. We lived on the west edge of the Spirit Lake School District. The schoolhouse was (and still is) on the southwest corner of Spirit Lake and to get there by road was three miles; walking through the woods and fields was only about one and a half miles. There was no transportation, so we walked across most of the time. There were five or six fences to get through, but if we kept going we could make it in about one half hour. School started at nine but the teacher always rang the bell at eight thirty, so you knew how much time you had. I remember in first grade it seemed like a long, long way and my sisters would keep rushing me. One morning I got mad and turned around and headed back home, but when I got within sight of the house, my Dad had seen me coming and met me. I don't remember anything he said, but he gave me a couple swats on my butt and turned me around and I went to school. I got there late, but never forgot it. That was getting an education from the bottom up.

I have so many memories of that walk to and from school. In the spring the beautiful wildflowers were indescribable. Mayflowers usually were the first, then Violets, Spring Beauty, Cowslips, Jack-in-the-Pulpits, just to name some. The teacher at least always acted as if she loved every bouquet she got, and sometimes every window available spot had a bouquet of

Carol about 1931.

7

flowers.

Another vivid memory I have is in the fall soon after school started, the leaves would turn all beautiful, then suddenly they would all come down and it would be like a new world with a beautiful carpet of all colors. When the winds came up they would blow them in piles so you could hide in them. Oh, the fun we had.

Then winter and snow and cold would come, and when a new snow would come we would have to break a trail. Usually the oldest would lead and we would follow, or we'd take turns breaking the trail. Sometimes if we had a weekend snowstorm Daddy had me take Bob (the horse) and ride him to break the trail. One time it had really been a lot of snow with a strong wind and some of the drifts were so deep, even the horse almost couldn't get through. Our path would pack down and build up so it was two or three feet above the ground. Then when spring started to come, and the snow was thawing, the path was still solid; if you could keep from slipping off one side or the other or both at the same time, you would end up sitting on the ridge with one leg on each side stuck in the wet snow. When you were little you probably needed some help to get up.

The woods in fall.

Then there were times when a blizzard would start during the day. Sometimes the teacher would let us out early so we could get home. I remember one time it was bad and we went a little of the way, then stopped at a neighbor's who would always give us lunch and we wasted so much time there it was getting dark before we got very far. The storm wasn't so bad in the woods but when we came out to the big field we had to cross, it was already dark and the snow was so thick and the wind so strong, we couldn't see 10 feet and wondered what to do. We almost decided to try to go back through the woods to the neighbor and then we heard a noise that we soon recognized: the dangling of trace chains. When horses pull anything there is always chains from whatever they are pulling fastened to the harness and they always make noise almost like a bell. When we heard that noise, we knew it was Daddy coming with the horses and sled to meet us. Boy, was that ever a good feeling. Then climbing into the hay in the box on the sled and sitting down under blankets and letting Dad and the horses bring you home. Oh what a good feeling of Security and Love that kids today seldom experience.

Another of the blessings of walking through the woods and across the fields to school was seeing the first robins and other birds in the spring. Hearing the first frogs in the spring, playing on the rubber ice, playing in all the little rivers as the snow was going off, or sampling the sap from the maple trees when they were tapped to make maple syrup in the spring.

Much of the haying in the 1920's and 1930's was done by first cutting it with the horse mower, then leaving it to dry. It was then raked with a 10 ft. horse drawn dump rake, then shocked by hand, and left to cure for a few more days. Then it was loaded by hand with a fork on to the hay rack which was pulled by horses and hauled to the barn where it was pulled up into the barn by a system of rope slings or a big hay fork pulled by the horses.

Hayfield in foreground, home in background, 1930's.

Dorothy, Carol, Pearl, Early 1930's, standing in creek close to house.

Cows standing in the creek close to house.

Mother Helen taking a picture.
About 1915.

Mother Helen with oldest daughter
Arlene. About 1918.

Dad's sister Hilive, Helen, Albert.

L-R: Sisters Loretta, Arlene, Bernice.
About 1923.

Top to Bottom: Raymond, Albert
(Dad), Agnes, Ida Helen (Mom).

Chapter Two: Spirit Lake School +

Spirit Lake School is one of the oldest schools in this part of Wisconsin. The first part was built in the early 1880's, and there was an addition put on sometime later. My Dad, my Mom, and many of my aunts and uncles went to school here, as well as the old time neighbors.

The school was going until the 1950's. It was never modernized. It had a water well you had to pump by hand, and a girls and boys outdoor toilet. It had a big old wood stove for heat. It did get electric lights in the early 1930's. It had one room, except in the end where you came in there was a short hallway about eight feet with the girl's coatroom on the left and the boy's on the right.

In the coatrooms were benches to sit on to put your overshoes, etc. on and hooks to hang your coats on and shelves to put your lunch boxes on. In the boy's coatroom was a two burner oil stove that was used in cold weather to heat water in a dishpan and the kids would bring cocoa, soup or whatever in jars that were set in the water with the lids loosened so they wouldn't explode when they heated up. This was the hot lunch program of those days. It was the teacher's job to appoint older kids to take care of these between first recess and noon. The cleaning, checking the toilets, carrying wood, doing the blackboards, etc. were all part of the teacher's job with the help of older kids. There was a water jug with about five gallons in the corner by the girl's coatroom.

There were good size windows down each side of the room; there were about five rows of seats and desks, about seven or eight in a row and benches along the walls. In the front the big stove was on the left, then the teacher's desk, and on the right, the class area with smaller chairs to sit on in class. It was all open to the whole school. So you could listen to and learn a lot from the older classes, as long as the teacher didn't see that you were paying attention to the class in

Spirit Lake School

front instead of your own studying or what you were supposed to be doing.

In the eight years I was in school, there were up to 44 kids and a low of 33 students. The teacher really had a big job, but I believe we kids learned more of what life is really all about than now. In my thinking the good teachers were the heroes of the day. They only got from about $60.00 to $100.00 a month for nine months, but jobs were very scarce, especially for girls, so with one year of teacher training, average intelligence and lots of determination, you could almost surely get a job. There was a country school almost every three miles or so.

I remember my first day in school very vividly when we walked in that first morning, that school looked so big. I remember the teacher sitting at her desk or standing in front. I even remember she had a beautiful white dress on. I didn't think of her being young then, but she must have been only 19 or 20 years old. She was the daughter of a neighbor. She had gone to school here for all of her eight years of school as well. She was a wonderful teacher and person. This was fall 1929 through winter & spring of 1930, my first grade in school. I remember what a big deal I thought it was when the calendar changed to the 1930's.

Carol with his teacher from the 1930's. Photo taken in 2003.

I have a lot of memories of those early 1930's; there were a lot of poor people, but as kids we never noticed it, probably because almost everybody was poor, but to me, eight or nine years old, they were exciting years. I loved horses, but I also loved cars, tractors, and machinery. And those were the years when cars, tractors, and machinery were changing and improving so much from year to year, in both looks and what they could do.

The county fairs were exciting to see the new tractors and cars. Almost every little town had two or three car and tractor dealers. They didn't have very many models on hand but they seemed to always have pictures of the new models that you could take home and look at. My Dad never bought a tractor until after I was in the Army in 1944. The first tractor in our neighborhood was a steel wheeled Fordson that the neighbor had. It was also power for the belt driven machines, such as silo filler, etc. I do remember Daddy getting some new horse drawn equipment, like a three horse sulky plow, and a field cultivator to name a couple. Anything new in those days was very exciting.

My lower grade school years went by without too much difficulty. I never had much of a problem learning. I did have quite a problem with my temper if I thought I or anyone else was being treated unfairly by the teacher or other kids. I would get mad trying to make things right. With forty kids or so, the teacher couldn't always know what was going on, but in our school there was some upper boys and girls that did a pretty good job of helping the teacher look out for the younger ones.

We really had a lot of fun walking to school and home, and also in recess and noon hour. In winter we did a lot of sliding. We never had a store bought sled, but my Dad made very good homemade sleds, skis and bobsleds, not only for us but also for neighbor's and relative's kids. There was a big hill by the school that was great. It was called the long hill; it was part of a discontinued horse and wagon trail. It had some curves so you had to be able to steer or you would go over in the deep snow. It was always a mad rush to get your clothes and overshoes on and get out there. If you were fast enough you could make two runs in a fifteen minute recess. This hill was right on our trail to walk to and from school and ended right down to the schoolhouse.

Carol, Dorothy, Pearl, about 1930. The first buck Dad shot, sitting with us on a bobsled he made.

In the fall and spring, we played ball and all kinds of games. The school grounds were only a few acres but we seemingly were allowed to play anywhere we could still hear the bell and get back in school in minutes, also we had to stay out of trouble. In those days there were three levels of discipline. First the teacher, if she didn't get satisfaction, she would call in someone from the school board to talk to the bad kids. If this didn't seem enough, they would call out the county superintendent of schools and he or she would come and lecture the problem students. I really don't remember very much discipline problems. There were a few. If a member of the school board or county superintendent was called in, the kids to be talked to were called into one of the cloakrooms to be talked to. The whole school would become very quiet. With everyone trying to hear what was being said, I believe it was quite effective.

I don't think I was a very troublesome student, but I found out what it was like once. A neighbor whose land joined the schoolyard had just dug a drainage ditch by hand in a swamp right near the school. There was peat bog that he dug out in big chunks and they laid up on the banks. A neighbor boy my age (about 8 or 9 years old) and I were playing along the ditch and we discovered it was so much fun to roll those big chunks of peat and let them splash back into the water in the ditch. The neighbor saw us doing it and reported it to the teacher. She decided to turn this over to the school board to handle. Well, it so happened my Dad was chairman of the school board and my friend's father was also on the school board, so they shouldn't be the ones to talk to us about us what's right and wrong to do. It took the third member of the school board to do it. I don't remember a thing he said but I think it was a good lesson.

About 1930.
Back L-R: Bernice, Arlene, Loretta.
Front L-R: Pearl, Dorothy, Carol.

In the fall of 1930, one morning when we came to school there was a new family starting school. They had just come from southern Missouri to the community by covered wagon, pulled by a horse and mule and the mother and older brother and young kids came along in a 1917 Model T Ford. Two brothers 11 and 14 and the oldest sister started out ahead with the covered wagon. Then the mother and older brother and younger kids started out with the car; after a while they caught up to the covered wagon and stayed with them for a few days, then they went on ahead and got here ahead of the covered wagon and got the place they had gotten to live in ready for the rest when they got there. This was the first day they had come to school. They were very poor, but good students. One of the boys was in my grade. We became good friends, all through school. Then, believe it or not, the oldest sister who helped her brothers drive that covered wagon pulled by the horse and mule from southern Missouri in a few years ended up my stepmother.

The 1930's had a lot of good happenings, but in my life there were some really sad happenings. On June 10th 1930 my mother had a baby girl. They named her June, I guess because she was born in June, but there was something wrong with her. The way I remember her, she was a nice little baby, but she was predicted not to live very long. She lived through the summer until school started in the fall. I guess I had learned to care a lot for her. I remember mother said I was usually the first one to ask how June was when we got home from school. Knowing she wasn't going to live long caused me as a young lad to do a lot of thinking about life, death, heaven, etc. Then we came home from school one day and Mom told us June had died. This was quite shaking for me. I will always remember that little casket in the living room. This was my first experience with death.

A highlight in 1930 was when my Uncle Milton and Aunt Freda and their kids (my cousins) came to visit from Saskatchewan, Canada. Aunt Freda was Daddy's sister and Uncle Milton grew up right close to our home. My grandfather homesteaded it in the early 1880's. Uncle Milton was a neighbor boy. They got married and homesteaded in Saskatchewan, Canada. He became a big wheat farmer. In 1928, he bought a new Reo Truck to haul wheat to market. He built a camper body on it in between planting and harvest, the whole family came to visit, Uncle Milton, Aunt Freda and all the eight or so cousins up to that date. That was quite a trip in that truck and homemade camper in those days. It was quite

Aunt Freda, Uncle Milton, cousins and family with the 1928 Reo Truck converted to a house on wheels.

the house on wheels at that time. The trip is a little over 1,000 miles one way, and not much blacktop road in those days. It was a very memorable time for us cousins to get to know each other. We had a lot of fun playing games, going fishing, doing the chores and doing the work that had to be done. There was no TV, very little radio, so we had to make our own fun, but we had a lot of it.

In the early 1930's, the economy was going from bad to worse, but us kids didn't notice it much. Our parents, and I think most parents, did very little complaining, at least not so we heard it. Most people worked very hard and did the best they could with what means they had. In those days, children didn't expect parents or government to make their life easy. Families worked together with everybody helping to make it better for all. As children we had to help even before we started school. I think as far as raising a family it was much better than now when so many kids seem to expect to have everything coming to them. My own feeling is that the bureaucracy, labor unions, and government laws that have been passed along with the welfare system and school system have made youth and adults too dependent on government. And in the process, much of our population doesn't know what a day of hard work is. I will be coming back to this once in a while down through the years.

Even though the times were hard in much of the country, there was a lot of progress from year to year in the automobile and machinery industry, and in the young boy who loved cars and tractors. We had a Model T Ford but all our farm work was still done with horses.

Spirit Lake School converted to a house in the 1960's.
Side door, porch and deck added about 1995.

Trade Lake Baptist Church, 1930's.

L-R: Dorothy, Loretta, Pearl.
About 1930.

Spirit Lake School class. Sister Dorothy is far left front.
About 1935.

Back L-R: Arlene, Bernice. Front L-R: Pearl, Dorothy, Carol. About 1936.

My father's sisters, Hilive, Augusta, and Frieda as young children. Late 1800's.

Back L-R: Uncle Pete Erickson, Albert (Dad), Ida Helen (Mother). Front L-R: Loretta, Carol, Arlene, Bernice. About 1925.

Chapter Three: Steam Power and Early Cars, Etc.

Steam Power

In the early days around 1880 to around 1930 most saw mills, thresh machines and early day factories were powered with steam engines. My grandfather was killed in a sawmill in 1894. He and my great grandfather did a lot of the threshing and lumber sawing in those days.

In the early 1900's, my Dad and two neighbor boys bought a sawmill and steam engine and went into the logging and lumber business. Daddy was 18 or 19 years old at that time and the neighbor boys were about the same age. I mention their age to show how in those days there was faith and trust in young people. My Dad told me how they took the train from Frederic to Minneapolis to make the deal. They paid $50.00 down on a new sawmill and a steam engine, then got back on the train for home and wondered if it would come. It did come in on a railroad flat bed in a couple of weeks. They operated for a few years but then went on to farming and other things, so there weren't any sawmills or steam engines in the family for many years. I have some really good memories of the late 1920's and early 1930's.

A sawmill with steam power moved in on the neighbors not far from our house. Every morning, noon, and evening they would blow the whistle. This was pretty exciting. Also, when the thresh machine would come in the neighborhood to do the threshing, you would hear the whistle blow and pretty soon you would hear the machine come clanking down the road. These were the days of steel wheels on machinery. They made a lot of racket on the gravel and rocky roads.

From the 1920's to the 1940's there was a gradual change replacing the steel wheels to rubber tires with air in them on tractors,

Lundeen's steam threshing machine.

wagons and farm equipment. Following is one amusing, yet sort of educational anecdote I have of those days that is so different from much of the thinking today. About the time gas service stations were putting in air compressors so you could put air in your tires free, this one old gentleman I remember with a Model T Ford from before 1920 would not use any of the free air because he didn't want anything that was free. I remember him pumping up one of his tires right close to where he could have put in free air. To me this was silly and ridiculous, but it was basically the way people thought: that you should work for what you got. I believe in those days all cars were sold with a hand tire pump and a patching kit, a jack and wheel wrench and a crank for the motor in case the battery went dead.

Steam threshing at Walter Wilson's.

In 1932, Henry Ford came out with the first V-8, this was really a car with a lot of go to it. A dream of any young boy was to have one someday. For most young fellows, even if you were old enough, the economy was so bad it was only a dream. There were some V motors earlier in the luxury cars. I think it was in the late 30's, some shirttail relatives of ours came visiting with a 1928 LaSalle with a V-12 motor. Wow, what a car, big and luxurious, but terrible gas mileage. But that first V-8 Ford was really the start of a lot of change in the car industry.

Also in 1932 was the beginning of the New Deal. As I have said before, as a child I really never realized how poor we must have been and I think my parents were somehow able to provide for us better than even some of our neighbors, so we didn't feel poor. Also I think our area was blessed with extremely hard working people. I also believe living in the northern rural area was a real advantage over living in the cities or the southern states where there was less change of seasons.

In this area most people lived on land where they could have a garden for vegetables, potatoes etc., and they canned and preserved food for the winter. There were a lot of wild berries in the woods. So most years you could pick wild berries, strawberries, blueberries, wild plums etc. that families together would pick and help can for the winter, besides having a feast of them in season.

Most families that I knew would have some animals like

cows, pigs, chickens etc. So in our case we usually had our own milk, butter and eggs and meat. The surplus was traded to the local grocery store for the things you needed to survive. My Dad always had three or four acres of wheat and we would get enough to take the best to the local flour mill and have our own flour for baking.

Late fall or early winter was butchering time. A beef steer or a poor milk cow, along with a nice hog was butchered for meat for the winter. These were exciting times for me because my Dad would designate me, the only boy at that time, to help my Uncle Richard butcher. He had been in the First World War and I guess he did a lot of butchering for the Army over in France. He was really good at it and because there were hardly any jobs to get, he went from place to place butchering wherever they wanted him. If I remember right he charged .50 an animal. He walked from place to place, usually making two or three places a day. In butchering season he would be so busy you couldn't always get him when you wanted him. Then Daddy would do it himself, but it took him a lot longer and he didn't like to do it. I learned enough so I could still do it, if need be.

Uncle (John) Richard Larson in WWI uniform in France.

I mentioned chickens for eggs but we also had chicken for dinner just whenever Mama would decide it should be on the menu. It usually had to be planned the night before when the chickens were roosting in the dark. As kids we were taught pretty young how to tell by feeling the bones on the rear of chickens where the eggs came out, if they were laying eggs or not. We would go in the chicken house in the dark and you could pick the chickens off the roost one at a time and feel if they were laying eggs or not. If they were, they were put back on the roost. If they weren't, we would put them in a crate until morning. Then next morning after chores, Dad (or one of us if he didn't have time) would take those chickens we had put in the crate the night before (usually two) and take them to the chopping block and chop their heads off. Next thing was to dip them in boiling water and then pick the feathers off. Then I think Mom took over. The next time we saw them was at dinner, and better roasted chicken I have never had.

Another blessing we had in this area was a lot of lakes with a lot of fish in them, so we would have a meal of fish quite often, mostly sunfish, crappies, and bass northern. We kids caught mostly pan fish. My memories of our fishing equipment was small tamarack trees cut in the swamp about one and a half inches on the bottom seven to ten feet long, tapered to about three-quarters of a inch in diameter. The bark peeled off and dried. A bottle cork with a slot cut in it with a jackknife to pull the line in to keep it at the proper depth. The only part that was bought was line, hook and sinker. We dug the angleworms for bait. Once in a while Daddy would go fishing for northern with a trolling line and spoon hook he would pull behind the boat. As he rowed around the lake, he would hold the line in his mouth so he could feel a bite. Both hands were on the oars. Sometimes he would take me along and let me hold the line; if a fish bit he would take the line and pull it in as fast as he could.

Another thing we had on the table almost every meal was homemade maple syrup. There were a lot of sugar maple trees in our woods and every spring we would tap trees and cook maple syrup. We would cook it down in a big pan and a cast iron thirty-gallon kettle, then Mom would can it. Pure maple syrup never spoils, so it can be kept for years.

Another thing that was a blessing to make a few dollars in the 1930's was the canning factory in Frederic that canned peas and beans, and a pickle factory in Grantsburg. The peas we harvested vines and all into the factory, but the beans, either green or wax, were contracted out 1/4 or more acres to whoever wanted a contract, some with cucumbers. You had to plant, weed, cultivate, and pick them, then bring them to the weigh stations to be weighed and paid for by the pound. There were different prices depending upon what grade they were, usually $.01 to $.03 per pound.

Usually as kids we would get $.01 per pound, and the rest would go to our parents or aunt for their part. It worked about the same for cucumbers. At home, we never saw money; it was saved to buy school clothes in the fall. So it was more fun to pick for Aunt Annie, even though we had to walk about two miles to her place, then pick all day. But she always gave us dinner, and in the evening when we brought the beans up to the house, she would weigh them and pay us cash on the spot, usually 25 pounds, so $.25, maybe up to $.75. Boy, what a haul $.75 was to me! Then we had to walk the two miles back home. I said this was a blessing, but sometimes working away in the hot sun, I'm not sure what we thought.

I talk of all these things we had, to help us live in spite of bad times, but also I believe all these things we did as the seasons of the year came, were also what made life interesting and because they were family affairs, taught us how to work, love and care for each other, and thank God for everything.

The good things we were enjoying weren't true all over the country. In the cities and in much of the south there was lack of jobs so many people were without enough food and clothes, even starving. The first national relief program I believe was started when Hoover was president. Someone came up with the idea if people just had seeds, they could plant a garden and grow some of their own food. So they distributed packets of seeds for people to plant. I think the idea was good, except that many people had never had gardens so didn't know how, and to make matters worse there was a drought, and most gardens never amounted to anything. So the project was mostly a failure.

Then in 1932, Franklin Roosevelt was elected President and he came up with the so-called New Deal. One of the programs he started to help poverty was WPA (Works Progress Administration). Villages, counties, schools, etc. could apply for government help to build schools, courthouses, even theatres to improve their area. Then people who needed jobs could get the jobs at these projects so they would have some income, but it was very poorly managed, so not much was accomplished for the hours worked, but at least they had to be on the job to get paid. So, looking back on it, I feel it was a better welfare program than now, where it is just handed out, like it has been for way too long now. I will get back to the New Deal and WPA later on in the later 1930's.

In the fall of 1933 tragedy struck our family for the second time. In those days there was no TV, and not too much radio. So there was more time for visiting

Carol mid-1930's.

and our family and relations got together a lot. Every birthday in the relation was celebrated. We had company that night, and as far as I knew, Mama was okay when she went to bed. In those days, because of the size of family, shortage of beds, etc., Mama and Pearl and Dorothy slept three in one bed. Daddy and I slept in one bed and my three older sisters Loretta, Bernice and Arlene in one bed upstairs. It was usual that Daddy, I and the three older girls would get up earlier and get the cows in and milk them. Mama would sleep in a little and then get up to get our school lunches ready and get breakfast ready for us when we came in to rush around and cleaned up, eat and get on our one and a half mile walk to school before nine o'clock, and we liked to get there early so we could have time to play before school or my sisters to help the teacher get everything on the blackboards etc. If it hadn't been for the help the teacher got from some of the older kids, I don't think she could have managed all she had to do for 40 students more or less and all eight grades in one room.

To get back to that tragic morning, the first one to get done milking their last cow would be the one to go to the house to get some warm water to rinse out the milk pails, separator, etc. Anyway, this morning it was Loretta who went to the house to get the warm water. She promptly came running back and screamed that Mama wasn't up. She was still in bed with Pearl and Dorothy, and she couldn't wake her. Then Daddy ran to the house to discover Mama was dead in bed. I don't remember much more of that day, except a lot of tears, and relatives and neighbors coming to support and help.

Daddy was fortunate to have three daughters aged 12, 14, and 16 years old to help. I was only 10 years old then, but still was a part of chores and help in every way. I was already driving the horses in the field at that time, and we didn't do it because we were expecting to get paid. It was just part of family life and it was satisfying and enjoyable. Nowadays kids expect so much. Even my own grandchildren, if you ask them to do something for you, are apt to reply with two questions. First, what is the job? Second, how much will you pay me?

In those days it was customary that after a death, the undertaker would prepare the body and bring it in the casket to your home and it would be in the best room in the house until the funeral. I can remember vividly Mama's beautiful casket in the parlor. This was the second memory of this as June's little casket was also in the house a day or two before the funeral. I remember the cold fall day of the funeral. We still had the 1926 Model Ford. It seemed like a long trip home from the graveyard. I remember as if it were only days ago. I also remember two ladies from church singing "He The Pearly Gates Will Open".

In 1930, the Trade Lake people, headed by Swanberg, the butter maker in the Creamery, decided they needed a bus to bring the students from the Trade Lake area into Grantsburg high school. I don't know the details, but they bought a New 1930 Dodge truck, just chassis, wheels 600 by 20 tires, engine and hood, no cab and somehow because of Daddy's experience working in Minneapolis in a street car body factory, he got the job to build a school bus onto this truck. The village blacksmith, Art Baker, and his father helped Daddy with the welding and iron work. Daddy was a super woodworker and metalworker, and as it was built mostly out of white oak framing, that was really something. They bought some used leather seats that were upholstered, so the seats were really comfortable. I think the sliding windows were from old streetcars. I must have been eight or nine years old, but I remember many a day that summer being helping dip screws

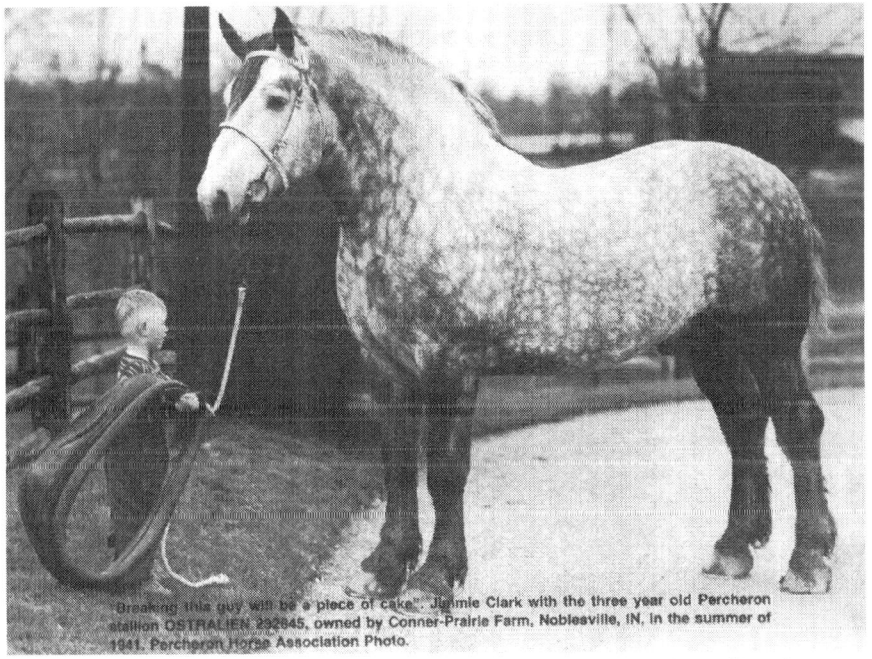

"Breaking this guy will be a piece of cake". Jimmie Clark with the three year old Percheron stallion OSTRALIEN 232945, owned by Conner-Prairie Farm, Noblesville, IN, in the summer of 1941. Percheron Horse Association Photo.

This picture is not me or any of our horses. It is out of a horse book. But it makes me smile and brings back memories every time I look at it; memories of when I was feeding, caring for, and harnessing the horses to get them ready to go out to work when I was so small I could barely reach. My sisters often accused me of using this as an excuse to get out of doing my share of milking the cows.
There may have been a little truth in this!

in paint before putting them in. I don't think Daddy ever put two pieces of wood together or put a screw in without paint between or on the screw. It must have paid off, because the school used that bus for years and then sold it to a Bible Camp that kept it going until only a few years ago. I think it is still around.

In those days some of the dependable seniors (maybe even juniors) in high school boys drove the school bus much of the time. Several drivers were out of high school, but still very young men. I don't know what they got paid but it was a good deal. Today, young people are not given a chance to show what they are capable of, lawmakers, lawyers, insurance companies, etc., in my mind are much to blame for the failure of our young people. Much of the peer pressure in those days was for good. Like a freshman seeing what the older students could do and trying to be as dependable as they were so hopefully someday he could sit in the drivers seat.

I believe it was 1934 when my sister Arlene got into teacher's training. In those days when you graduated from high school, you could go into teachers training right by the high school, and in one school year you were a teacher. There were some complications with riding the bus for some reason, and by then Bernice and Loretta were also in high school. So Daddy bought a 1926 Model T Ford Coupe for $20.00 for Arlene to drive to school. She had that car and drove about fifty miles on Sunday afternoon to her teacher's job at Lee school and stayed with people close to school until Friday after school, when she and a couple of other girls would come home.

I have so many memories of that car and my Dad teaching Arlene to drive in the family Model T. That one had something wrong so you could lift the steering wheel off. Daddy never had problem with it because he was tall, but Arlene was short and so when she put her foot on the brake she would unintentionally lift up on the steering wheel. One Sunday afternoon we were going to visit Dad's Uncle Erickson about seven miles from home and Arlene was getting a driving lesson at the same time the whole family was in the car. We weren't going fast but we came over one hill and started down another one;

1926 Model T Ford Coupe.

she must have reached her foot for the brake, anyway she pulled the steering wheel off and the car went off to the right down through a farmers barnyard before we stopped. Daddy got the car back on the road and fixed the fence a little and we went on to Uncle Erickson's. What do you know, on the way home he still had her driving, and on a bigger hill she did it again and we were heading off a big bank, but Daddy got his foot on the brake and his strong finger got a hold of the end of the shaft the steering wheel fit on so he kept it from going over the bank until he got it stopped. She did learn to drive and drove that Model T Coupe for several years and then sold it for $40.00.

I have so many memories of that Model T Coupe. All six of us would cram into it and head for Sunday school as fast as it would go because we didn't get started as early as we should have. In the Model T's of that time a gas pedal on the floor was an extra, otherwise it was only on the steering rod. This one was foot fed; it worked okay most of the time, but sometimes it would stick so you had to pull it back up by hand.

One Sunday we came home from Sunday school and Arlene pulled up by the shed door where both cars were garaged. She was going to let us out of the car and then drive in, because when you drove in there was only about eight feet between the two cars on one side and on the other side a post and all kinds of machinery. So it was hard to get in or out of the shed. There were two lumber piles in front of the cars about four feet high and four feet wide straight up except for a little pile scattered in front. Anyway, we were just about to open the door to get out. I don't know if one of us kids hit the foot feed or what but all of a sudden that Model T took off flying into the shed. It missed the other car on one side and the post and stuff on the other and hit that lumber pile in front. Daddy never could figure out how it could do it, but the front wheels went straight up the side of that lumber pile and stopped with the front wheel right on top of the side of that lumber pile and against the wall of the shed. It looked like it was almost standing on end, but we were okay. It was a miracle none of us had started to get out or we might have been crushed between the cars. I don't know how Arlene explained that to Daddy.

I think that Model T had something to do with the fact I didn't go to high school, not entirely but maybe something. School came quite easy for me but I never really enjoyed being in school rather than working on the farm or whatever. After Mama died, Daddy and I did a lot together and he intentionally or not built such a love for our home and farm that I didn't think I ever wanted to be anywhere else. I couldn't see that I needed high school, and here's where the Model T Coupe came into the picture. On cold mornings he would have to get it started so they could go to high school and sometimes that was a project! Evidently the clutch on those cars when it was completely released, and so the practice was to jack up one back wheel, then it would crank easier.

There was no self-starter, if it was really cold you would get a pan of hot coals and put it under the engine and transmission to warm it up. It was rather hazardous to put it close enough up to bottom of the engine to warm it up like you wanted it to, but not so close that the car would catch on fire. Some cold mornings Daddy would work cranking that Model T and doing everything to hopefully get it going (and usually he did) that he would get quite upset about how much trouble it was to get those girls to high school.

I really did enjoy those years working on the farm. I have always said there was nothing quite as peaceful as riding on the Sulky Plow behind three big horses, the only noise the clanking of the trace chains and the soft cracking of the

Carol cutting hay.

ground as the furrow turned over, and stopping occasionally to rest the horses and pet them. Also to enjoy the lunch usually brought out to you mid morning and mid afternoon. I am getting ahead of the times here because this didn't happen until about 1936 to the early 1940s before I went in the Army.

It must have been not too long after Daddy bought that Model T for Arlene that he traded the family 1926 two-door for a 1929 Model A Tudor with a trunk on the back that was bought as an accessory. It was a very useful addition. I was really proud of this car.

Albert (Dad) in front of the 1929 Model A
Tudor. One of the girl's bonnets
is in his hand.

Cousin Harland Brask, Carol,
1930's.

L-R: Carol, Pearl, Arlene, Loretta, Dorothy,
Bobby in front. About 1936.

L-R: Carol, Pearl, Dorothy holding Bobby.
About 1936.
Note the lunch pail in Carol's hand.

Gardening, about 1938.
Loretta, Pearl, Dorothy, Bobby.

The Richter Family.
L-R Back: Rob, Hardy, Ellis, Gladys (my step-mother), Dick, Jack.
Lolita is in front.

Chapter Four: The Thirties

After Mama died, it was really hard. The older girls were in high school and the rest of us were in grade school. I'm not sure if Pearl had started school yet or not. Daddy had a lot of outside responsibility, such as County Commissioner, Trade Lake Fire Insurance Company president, School Board etc. Jobs were very scarce for girls unless you took teachers training and even then you couldn't be sure of a job. Anyway, Gladys Richter, the oldest of the family that had moved in from Missouri, needed a job and Daddy and our family needed help. I don't know what the salary agreements were, but she came to help and live with us. She was a very capable, hard working young lady, just what Daddy and my older sisters needed. I remember very little of that winter but her looks and ability to cook, wash and mend clothes, work outside, or whatever was needed must have swept Daddy off his feet, because on April 27th 1934, they were married.

I had a lot of mixed feelings. She was great in every way except I maybe thought she was too Scotch in some ways. We were poor and she was very conservative. We had all we wanted as far as bread, potatoes, milk, etc., but when it came to cake, cookies, and meat, we got our one piece and that was it. She kept the cookies hidden, and she knew how many were left and if you found them and took one, you were in trouble. The only other thing I sort of resented was that because Daddy had a new love, he had less time for me.

From the early 1930's through 1936 or 1937 were not only bad times as far as financial problems but were the driest years that I remember. It was so dry there was a real shortage of hay and all crops. I remember how Daddy kept us cultivating the corn as deep as we could to bring up moisture to keep it growing.

In the 1930s was the first I heard about unions. The price of milk was so bad, the farmers got together and started an organization called Farmers Union to try to get prices up on milk and farm products. They tried to get all dairy men to not sell their milk so it would force the price up. I don't know how much good it did, but I remember we couldn't sell our cream, so we made butter out of it in our old fashioned churn. This milk strike got pretty wild, so there were roadblocks and fights. It was pretty scary. Daddy was not a Farmers Union man. He believed there were better ways, but if you knew my Dad, he got himself involved.

On our farm and in our area there are a lot of wet meadows that are boglike that you can't drive on, but meadow hay did grow there and it was better than nothing for feed. Daddy would get some help and cut this hay by hand with a scythe. I couldn't keep up with the men, but I tried. It was kind of fun because you were allowed to be wading in the water with your shoes on.

When you cut with a scythe the hay ends up in a ridge of hay called a windrow and left to dry. The long stubble would hold up out of the water, then in a day or two you would go and put it in shocks with forks and wooden racks with wood teeth about four inches long. The shocks would be left to dry a few days, then we would make stack bottoms out of brush to keep the hay from getting down in the swamp so it would get wet. We had two smooth poles ten feet or so in length that we would push under the shocks about two feet apart. The poles would stick out on each side of the shock so one man on each end would take the end of the two poles, one in each hand, and both would lift up and carry the whole shock to the stack. The stack would be carefully made to shed water and it would be left there till winter when we could take the sled and horses and drive on the meadow because it would be frozen hard and snow covered. We went right out there with the horses and sled with the hayrack on it and hauled the hay home to feed the cattle.

In those years before pesticides, there were other almost plagues. I remember one year the army worms were really bad in the more sandy areas. Army worms would somehow get started and get to be so thick they would work just below the top of the ground and eat everything as they went. We never had them at home but I remember Daddy took us along to see where they were working, and it was just bare ground. There must have been millions of them, because they would work almost in a straight line, taking a swath one half mile or however long even across the sandy roads. You could hear them chewing away. Where they had been, all vegetation was gone, it was all brown. In our immediate area it never was bad, but it created a big scare.

One of very special things after Daddy remarried was when Gladys, my

Carol with Bobby, about 1936.

stepmother, had a baby and it was a boy. So I had a brother. Until then all I had was sisters, so to have a brother was really great and I could hardly wait until he grew big enough to do things with me.

In 1935 I was twelve years old, soon a teenager and big enough to drive even the big three-horse hitch machinery in the field; that was great. I wasn't very big, so it was quite a job to be able to reach to get the harness on etc. Harnessing horses is hard to explain unless you have some knowledge of how it's done, but I have a vivid memory of one time I came in from the field with those three big horses. First you had to unhitch from whatever equipment you were using, and then drive the horses up to the barn door. Then you had to separate them so they could go through the barn door one at a time. This amounted to tying up the driving lines and hooking up the cross lines. The last thing was to get the check line (this was a line from the bit that goes in the horse's mouth and over one of the hames, which was the highest part, this line was so the horse couldn't put his head too far down). The check line had to be taken off from behind the hame so the horse could put his head down enough to get through the barn door. Anyway, I could hardly reach to do this and I was stretching and trying to do this, unaware that anyone else was around, so it scared me when somebody that I hadn't seen said "if you would put a piece of paper under your feet maybe you could reach". Grandpa Richter had walked up and I didn't know he was there. Grandpa Richter with his dry humor and other things was a guy to remember. The first years they lived up here he still worked in Chicago and only came home once in a while.

The summer of 1935 was the year Daddy and my new mother decided to take a trip. They hadn't had a honeymoon so I guess this was a combination honeymoon and visit to his sisters and families in Saskatchewan, Canada. My brother Bobby was a baby in diapers and still nursing, so he had to go along. Why we will never know, but they decided to take my sister Bernice and me along. Our car was that 1929 Model A Ford Tudor. There wasn't much room, with Daddy driving, Gladys holding Bobby in the front

Threshing.

Carol with Wade Brask and George Larson
by Carol's Allis-Chalmers/Rumley tractor

seat, suitcases, boxes, etc. on the floor and in the middle in the back seat. Bernice and I had just barely enough room to sit, one on the right side and one on the left, with all the stuff between us. We could hardly see each other but we could talk. I always thought they took the two of us along because we were the most apt to get in a fight. Bernice would get more upset than the other girls, so I loved to tease her.

The trip was about one thousand miles, quite a trip for a Model A Ford in those days. We traveled across Minnesota to Fargo, North Dakota, then northwest across North Dakota through Minot, and into Canada. Our relatives farmed not too far into Canada, above Montana.

The first day we started early, but had trouble with the carburetor on the car so lost some time, but Daddy kept on going until he was weaving all over the road because he was so tired. Finally Gladys got him to stop and we slept in the car until morning. Next day, we made about one half of the rest of the way and rented a little cabin for the night. The next day we got there.

There are a few things I especially remember about this trip. Those were before the days of Pampers, so when Bobby needed a change Gladys would put a dry one on him, then if the one she took off was just wet, she would pin it above the window on the door on her side, then she would lower the window enough to put the diaper out and then crank up the window and it would blow out there until it was dry. Then she would take it in, fold it up and it was ready for the next time (this worked really well).

Another thing I remember is the alkali flats and smells, and the water was terrible. I guess it was worse because the country was so dry, but we could hardly handle it. Another thing was the dust. It was real dry and mostly all dirt roads. So there was always a cloud of dust behind you and every car you met you would be blinded with the dust for a while, and it would almost make you choke. If Gladys had a diaper drying out the window and saw a car approaching she would quick roll down the window to get the diaper inside and roll the window back up quickly, or the diaper would get dirty from the dust. The dust from our car went backwards, so it wasn't a bother.

We did have a great time in Canada for about a week, I had four boy cousins from a little younger than me to a little older. And Bernice had three or four girl cousins around her age. I spent my time with the boys and her with the girls, so I don't remember seeing much of her that week.

Uncle Milton had already progressed, so instead of cutting the wheat with a grain binder, shocking it, then hauling it to the thresh machine to thresh, he had a 16' cut ground driven combine. A ground driven combine machine is one that has a big bull wheel with big cleats on it that had a big sprocket on it and sprocket chain to other shaft chains, shaft bearings, etc., to make every part of the machine run when you put it in gear. There were no mounted power units on it as there are on combines today. The combine was pulled with his 18-36 Rumley oil pull tractor. He had two of these, the first bought in 1915, the second I am not sure when.

Up until 1915, Uncle Milton was farming entirely with horses; he was planting hundreds of acres of wheat with horses. In 1935 when we were there, he had a thousand or more acres of wheat. He had those same tractors until after we were there. In 1935, he traded for two John Deere tractors and two 10' combines instead of the old 16'. Because it was so dry, the crop was very poor that year; the yield was only about eight bushels per acre. It was really fun to ride on that big combine as they were harvesting. One thing I remember was the night before we left for home. Uncle Milton asked me how I liked it out there, and I said I liked it but I thought I liked Wisconsin better if we just didn't have to pull teats (milk cows) morning and night. And he said: "If I get one good crop every seven years, I'll make more money then you ever will pulling teats".

Another memory is of going to get the cows on horseback. They had a few cows for their own

In front of Uncle Albert Anderson's house, 1935. L-R: Albert (Dad), Gladys holding Bobby, Carol, Bernice, Uncle Albert.

needs of milk, butter and meat. They had one little saddle horse. They let me go along because I was company. It was a long lane with the pasture in the end of the lane where there was some lower land with little grass. My cousins would have a problem deciding who should go to get the cows and take me along.

Another of my Dad's sisters, Aunt Augusta and Uncle Albert, lived a few miles from Uncle Milton. Uncle Albert was still farming on a smaller scale with horses. We stayed there some too. One morning they gave me the job to get the horses out of pasture again. It was a long lane, then pasture both to the right and left of the lane in some rough ravine country. I thought I walked miles both ways and never found the horses and was about to give up when Daddy and Uncle Albert came out there with the car to see what happened to me. We finally found the horses in a low spot I had missed.

In those days in Canada, the Dakotas etc., they usually only took one crop every other year off the land. They would farm in strips, one strip would have wheat on it, and the next strip was cultivated every so often all summer. The next year this strip would have the crop on and the one with the crop on this year would be idle. They called this summer following.

There were several families in that area that had moved from Wisconsin in the early 1900's and many were shirttail relatives of my Dad. So we had a lot of visiting to do and I remember going to one place where they still lived in a sod house. It didn't look like much on the outside, but was really cozy and nice inside. Sometimes I think the women of the pioneer days were really the heroes for their hard work and ability to make things comfortable, beautiful, etc. with not much to do it with. Besides helping outside whenever needed and doing the cooking, washing, mending clothes, etc.

Threshing with steam power.

I remember the last Sunday we were there, Aunt Freda and Uncle Milton invited everybody over for a meal and to visit. It was pretty big bunch. They had a sing a long in the afternoon. I remember singing

36

God Save the King etc. If my memory is correct it seems Bernice could play guitar and they had one for her to play and she tried to lead in singing some patriotic songs we knew. It was okay, but I remember some cousins made fun of some of the songs we sang, and I got real mad about it. The next morning we left for home, and I have really no memories of the trip home.

It must have been in 1936 that Gladys gave birth to my first half sister, Florence. I don't know what the problem was but Gladys got terribly sick. It seemed she maybe wouldn't live. It was a really bad time for Daddy and all of us. I will always remember one hot afternoon, some of my sisters and I were helping to shock hay on what we called the big long field. Daddy came home from seeing Gladys at the Grantsburg hospital and told us they didn't know if she would live. I don't know any of the details, but Daddy wasn't satisfied with what they were doing for her in Grantsburg. And he had a lot of faith in Dr. Arverson from Frederic hospital, so he took her to Frederic. I don't know much about it, but it made the difference and she was soon okay and back home, gaining strength, and getting back to her old self.

At St. Croix Falls, 1936. Back: Bernice, Carol. Front: Dorothy, Arlene holding Bobby, Loretta, Pearl.

Special revival meetings once a year or so were very much a part of many churches, I think especially so back then. Sometimes churches would go together and rent a big tent and get the best evangelist they could, and would draw big crowds. The preaching was powerful. Fire and brimstone, Heaven or Hell told in no uncertain terms. The music and singing of those old hymns would really ring out across the countryside. It was really moving and people were saved.

I was saved at special meetings in our church, in the summer of 1936 and was baptized in Wood Lake at the Bible Camp. It was the most important decision of my life but at that time I wasn't very sure what it meant. Growing up in Sunday school, I always took it pretty seriously, and some of those Old Testament accounts really bothered me. I will always remember one Sunday in Sunday School we had a lesson in the Old Testament where it seemed God decided to destroy thousands of people for their wickedness. I felt this was unfair, especially to the children, and I just couldn't understand if God loves everyone how he could do this. I became so angry I went home not sure I wanted to have anything to do with God. I got over it, but all my life I have been working at sorting out these things. Perhaps later on as we go through the years and the trials of my life, I will talk more of my faith in God and what I believe.

Trade Lake, 1930's.

Trade Lake Creamery, about 1915.

Chapter Five: Steam, Gas, and Diesel

Steam-Gas-Diesel

From before 1900 even, there were a lot of brilliant minds trying to build a good steam car. A lot of them were built from the 1900's into the 1930's; some of them were pretty good. Steam power is about the nicest power there is. The problem is, there has to be some kind of fuel burned to create the heat to make the steam. Steam traction engines were very popular for power for threshing machines, saw mills, etc., because there was lots of wood available to fire with to heat up the water in the boiler.

Steam engines were almost the exclusive power for trains all the way back into the 1800's. For one thing, no other power had been invented as good and strong. The other thing was they could pull a carload of wood or coal behind the engine to fire with. The train always had an engineer and a fireman. It was the fireman's job to hand feed the firebox under the boiler to keep the steam up so it could pull the train. It was not a job you needed a college education for, but you really had to know what you were doing. In 1910 or 1911, Daddy worked on the railroad as a fireman. He had many stories of his experiences there, pulling those trains in the mountains.

Most trains were pulled by steam engines until the late 1930's when the big diesel locomotives began replacing them. I thought this was sad, because it was great to hear that whistle blow when the train went through, even though we lived about ten miles away, or to be in town at the depot waiting for it for someone or some freight coming in. The sound of the steam locomotive and the whistle was so much more exciting than the diesel that replaced it.

The steam car idea stayed very much alive until in the 1930's; some of them were quite successful. A neighbor machinist and steam fan that used to do work for us worked on a steam car engine many years until he died. There probably still are some people trying. The problem with steam power is that you have to have water and some kind of fuel along or replenish too often. Then as gas engines improved, steam cars just couldn't compete. Farm tractors were mostly powered by gasoline until in the late 1930's, diesel farm tractors started coming in. For me, it was an exciting concept that an engine could fire and run without spark plugs.

The first engine I remember us having was a three horsepower International with big flywheels that started on gas, and then when it warmed up you could run it on kerosene. We used it to saw our firewood and power for Daddy's homemade woodworking machines or any belt driven machine such as a bean thresher or seed cleaner, but he soon got these running with electric motors. In those days most of the water was pumped with small single cylinder gas engines or windmills until they got electricity.

In those days, we sold cream to the creamery in Trade Lake. The creamery burned wood to make steam for their steam engine that ran the machinery and made hot water steam for washing everything, so every fall they would have what they called a wood auction. They wanted to buy say 100 cords of wood, so they would bid it in five or ten cord lots. Instead of bidding up you would bid down. The auctioneer would say how much a cord would you cut ten cords for and deliver it. The first bidder would say, maybe $12.00 a cord, the auctioneer would ask who will do it for less. So the low bidder would get the contract to cut and deliver for whatever amount he bid.

Sawing wood.

Daddy would usually bid for ten to twenty cords for us to cut and deliver in the winter. We sawed with a two man cross cut saw and split it, it was three foot long wood. We could haul one cord on the sled to the creamery about two and a half miles when there was snow on the roads. I have some cold memories of that job. It was easy going with the load because the horses would walk so if you got cold you could walk beside the sled, but then when you got down there you would have to unload by hand one piece at a time. By this time the horses would have cooled off and you were probably sweating from working hard unloading. Horses always are in a hurry when they know they are headed for home, and our horses were always big (1,500-1,750 lbs.) animals and fast and hard in the mouth. So on the way home you had to sit on the front of the sled with your feet braced, pulling the lines for all you were worth to hold the horses from running away home. So by the time you got home you were just about frozen.

Several winters there were two other projects Daddy did

to make a little more money. In the fall and into the winter, he would build wooden snowplows with a grader bit on the bottom and a steel runner that kept it from going sideways. These plows would go alongside horse drawn sleds pulled with two or four horses, depending on how much snow there was to plow. Most townships didn't have any power snowplows, so they could buy these homemade snowplows, and get different farmers to take care of a few miles of roads. If it was too deep we would have to shovel through the big drifts, but Daddy made a few of these plows several different winters. There were some other men who made some plows to, but the ones he made were rounded like the steel plows of today so they rolled the snow better, so were in demand.

Also, Daddy built the best wooden rowboat that I ever seen. In my estimation they were the easiest rowing boats ever, besides being built so well and out of good lumber so they would last almost forever if you took care of them. They were in demand and he would usually take on to build more of them than he could do to be ready for summer fishing. So sometimes we would be working way into the night and into the

Rowboat.

spring, when we should have been planting corn etc., but we had to get the boats done to live up to his word. These boats had paint between every place where 2 pieces of wood went together, and there were no nails. It was all screws and every screw had to be dipped in paint before it was put in. In those days there were no power screwdrivers; there were hand screwdrivers or what they called speed drills or screwdrivers, but no electric or air drivers.

I will never understand how Daddy could accomplish all the things he did, both at home and his outside jobs. I said we sometimes did things when maybe we shouldn't have, but I did help and at least most of the time really enjoyed it. In those days, parents expected their kids to help, and somehow they put love and respect into it, so you never wanted to or dared to go against their will.

Daddy did have a hired man, Phillip, a lot of the time in the early 1930's. Good wages for a hired man in those days was $1.00 a day plus meals. He usually came around 7:00 to 8:00 am and went home after supper, around 6:00 pm. Daddy worked a

Hunting license from 1938.

lot more hours than that. Phillip had a 1926 Star car (a coupe) that I think he bought new and I think he drove it until 1939, when he bought a new Ford V-8.

One thing I remember about those days was that the townships paid bounty for gophers, woodchucks, etc. I guess it was because it was so dry and they were hard on the crops, but I think it was also a sort of help for kids or anyone to make a little money. So I trapped mostly gophers; they paid $.10 a head when you brought them to the town chairman. I remember Phillip getting almost upset, because some days I made just as much money trapping gophers as he did working all day.

Another thing that was an important part of my life in the 1930's was 4-H. 4-H clubs are still going today, and I think they are a very good thing for young people, but they were an even greater part of life in the 1930's when there was no television, etc. You could have a project of your and your parent's choice, a calf, sheep, chickens, gardening, potatoes, or whatever. You would have a record book to fill out as your animal or vegetables grew. Then at County Fair time, you would bring your animals or produce from your garden to be judged. The judging was for a price in dollars, not much, but in those days it seemed like a lot.

The County Fairs were always a very special time of year in the 1930's. The excitement of the Fair was really something. You could sometimes stay overnight to take care of your animal. One memory I have of this is the time I and a couple of other boys stayed overnight, and we made pancakes for breakfast (big, soggy ones, Uffda!). I was so full of pancakes! The Fair was run mostly by volunteer help, and my Dad sold tickets at the gate. In those days, airplanes were just getting popular, and often there would be one or two willing to take people up for a ride for $1.00. Daddy gave me the money, and said go for a ride. What a thrill, my first airplane ride! You never know how beautiful the country is until you see it from the sky. It was

4-H Picnic held at our house, 1930's.

great, but all of a sudden, those pancakes wanted out. I had a handkerchief in my overalls, so i puked into it and threw the handkerchief and all out the window. I wonder if anyone found it.

It must have been in 1937 that Daddy traded the 1929 Model A Ford, for a 1933 Ford Tudor (suicide doors) This car really had a lot of pep and was fun to drive. I had a drivers permit to drive to the creamery when I was 13. Our family and two neighbors took turns hauling the cream to the creamery. We also hauled the cream for a couple of old maid sisters who had no car, and somehow it got to be a habit for them to have me, my Dad, or whoever went, to pick up groceries for them. They would send a grocery list and some money and you would have to shop for them. This I didn't like but I had no choice. When Dad said do it, you did it!!! To get all the cream cans and egg cases and everything in you had to take out the back seat. These old maids really tried to be friendly and insisted I come in for cake and milk. They weren't very good cooks. I remember having a monster piece of cake, really heavy and some kind of frosting that tasted like sour cream or something, but they would insist I cleaned it up.

Arlene and friends by 1933 Ford Tudor.

Frank Larson plowing with Ned and Nellie on the Albert Peterson farm near Trade Lake, Burnett County, 1921.

On creamery morning (Monday/Wednesday/Friday), the Village of Trade Lake usually would have several horse drawn rigs and a lot of cars of that time, so it was a busy town. There were two stores, a meat market, creamery, feed store, garage, blacksmith shop, and two or three taverns. The hotel building was still there but it was closed. The Trade Lake Town Hall is still in use and almost the same as it was then.

There was a dam and millpond and water-powered feed and flourmill (Trade River ran right through town). After the creamery association built a feed store, this other one closed up. Then sometime in the 1940's, the dam went out and there was no longer a millpond. We really had lots of good times skating on the millpond. One of the Baker boys (blacksmith's son) was a really good skater and he would clean the snow off and often make a fire. Then a girl that lived in Trade Lake would call up and I and my sisters Dorothy and Pearl would go down skating, and three of my cousins who lived close would come, and it was great. I would skate with my cousin's sisters but especially this one girl called up, especially when it was moonlight. Oh, she was a good skater, and beautiful too. I guess maybe my dream of a girlfriend, but I was so bashful that's as far as it got.

For some reason in those years there were a lot of girls in my life. Lots of sisters and cousins and more special ones after I got my drivers license and could get the car to go roller skating or a movie, as long as I would take my sisters along and my cousins. Dad and Uncle Frank had faith in me so he would let us take his car if I promised to drive and behave. If I could manage it, that good skater would also be along. Those were some good times.

My sister Loretta was a couple of years older than me. In the fall of 1937, she was 17 years old and a senior in high school. She was very smart, beautiful and kind, besides being a poet. In the fall, it seemed she was always tired. I still have guilt feelings because of complaining that she couldn't seem to hold up her end doing chores, etc. By Christmas time she was quite sick but she never complained, just kept on doing the best she could as far as helping at home, and kept up being a super student in high school, besides writing poems and reading and clipping poems that others wrote, putting them in a scrap book.

Here is a poem by Ella W. Wilcox that she had in her scrapbook:

Loretta's class, Loretta is third from right in back.

*I know there are no errors
In the great eternal plan.
And all things work together
For the final good of man.
And I know when my soul speeds onward,
In its great eternal quest,
I shall say as I look back earthward
Whatever is - is best.*

Here is a poem that Loretta wrote called "The Blessings of Rain", that won first prize in a contest:

*O beautiful rain which our God hath sent
We may not know yet what your coming has meant
But we'll have good hope and maybe we'll see
A year full of bountiful blessings from thee.*

*Your touch is so gentle, so cool, and so sweet,
As you generously fall on the plants at our feet.
A new hope for the future you inspire in me,
A hope which comes only from blessings as thee.*

*As I listen I hear on the roof up above
A patter like music which tells of God's love.
'Tis long that I listen and loud that I sing
Of the peace and the hope which this pattering brings.*

*Now the grass is much greener on the hills all around
And I know of some seeds sprouting down in the ground
Which early in springtime about us we sow;
But without rain and sunshine they would never grow.
And then at the dawning a rainbow I see
Its meaning is not just in colors to me
But a soft hopeful whisper comes down through the trees
"'Tis the end of a rain, but a sign of God's peace."*

She was the greatest in every way. Everyone loved her; it seems she was just too angel-like to be on this earth. She went to the hospital around Feb. 1st, 1938 and died Feb 25th. Daddy was with her when she was dying and she talked about heaven and all the beautiful flowers and seeing our mother and baby sister June. She died sometime in the night and Daddy came home and woke us up and told us about her beautiful death.

May, 1937 was also the year I graduated from 8th grade. What a milestone, all done with school. Wow, now I was ready to take on the world. I had more dreams and hopes than you can imagine, and enthusiasm. As I said before, I never had it hard in school, but I had so much love for the home place I couldn't see wasting any more time going to school. So I had my mind made up that I wasn't going to high school. I think Daddy was partly to blame because he complained sometimes how hard and expensive it was to keep those sisters of mine in high school. I remember it was a beautiful summer working in the fields and gravel pit, going fishing, etc. I had said I wasn't going to high school. Daddy would say I think you'll change your mind by fall, but he didn't say that I had to. So fall came and it was time to start high school. Daddy said, you are going, I said I am not going. He said yes you are; I said no I'm not. He finally said if you go three weeks and still want to quit, then you can. I said OK, but three weeks will be it.

The first day I didn't get ready in time so I missed the bus. The bus made a kind of loop around by Trade Lake so Daddy said you get on your bike and ride and ride for all you're worth and you catch the bus west of home by Ryss Blacksmith Shop. I knew I'd better do what he said. I missed the bus at the corner, but because it had to stop a couple times to pick up kids, I managed to catch it about a half a mile down the road. I left my bike in the brush in the ditch and got on the bus and went to school. I got off the bus that night in the same place, and rode my bike home. I really kind of liked high school, so by the time the three weeks were up, it was a hard decision, but I still thought my time was worth more at home and besides, I was a man of my word and I had said I would quit, so I did. I don't remember Daddy giving me a hard time about it, but the high school principal did every time we saw each other until he died.

Family 1942. Back L R: Arlone in front of Carol, Bernice, Dorothy, Pearl. Front L-R: Bobby, Gene, Florence, Muriel, Alice.

Trade Lake Town Hall

Photo of the lake taken in 1938 by Loretta.

Family 1950.

47

Trade Lake Church

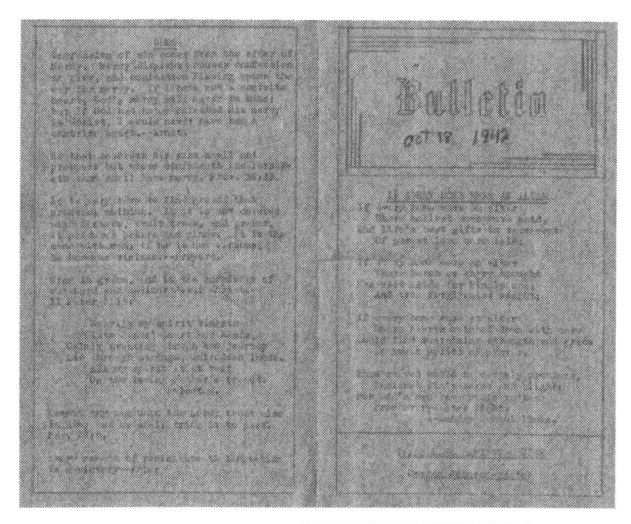

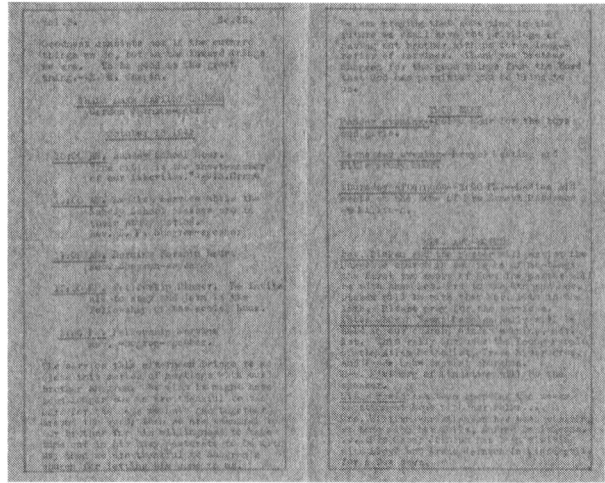

Chapter Six: Rumors of War and Army Days

Those years from 1937 to the early 1940's, I worked hard on the home farm and in the gravel pit with Daddy and my stepmother Gladys to keep from losing the farm, but I don't remember being unhappy about it or feeling sorry for myself or us, or blaming my parents, the government or God. We were just happy to be able to try to make our mark in this world and to promote the Love of God and Country.

The late 1930's were also when Hitler thought he was going to rule the world and develop a Super Race and murder the Jews; also, Italy, Russia and Japan were all causing a lot of trouble. I think I was a very serious young fellow and it really bothered me why, if God is really in control, why he allowed it to be this way. This has bothered me a lot down through the years why it so often seems life is so unfair.

I have never been to Bible College, but as a child, besides Sunday school, we usually attended one or two summer Bible Schools. One of the best things about these Bible schools was memorizing. Memorizing came quite easy for me and I am very thankful for what I memorized. It has helped me all my life, but the starving, dying children and people all over the world, the thousands killed needlessly in war etc., also natural tragedy and bad things in your families or life, are really hard to take. In Genesis, when God threw Adam and Eve out of the garden and gave them the knowledge of good and evil he also gave them control of their lives. So that unless they were really God's children what happened to them was not necessarily God's Plan, but because of our own faults and because the devil is the Prince and Power of this world. I may touch on these thoughts again some time down through the years.

To get back to the late 1930's and the threats and start of the Second World War. I didn't turn 18 or draft age until 1941 and the war was in full swing. We were farming pretty big, we thought, for that time, and Daddy had so many jobs, such as town chairman, Insurance President, etc. etc. Anyway, my family thought they needed me and I guess I thought so, too. I was deferred until 1944.

The years from 1940 to 1944 when I went in the Army were great years even though I had guilty feelings for not being in the service after I turned 18 in 1941. I worked really hard on the farm,

1931 Model A Ford Coupe.

in the gravel pit, sawing lumber, and helping the neighbors all we could, too. I think it's hard to describe if you didn't experience those years when it was quite uncertain what the outcome of the war would be and if the loved ones and friends you knew were in it would ever come home again. I had just turned 18 and bought my first car a 1931 Model A Ford Coupe for $85.00. Gas was rationed, so we couldn't drive too much, but with a lot of beautiful girls around, it was great. We did quite a bit of rollerskating in the summer and ice skating in the winter, besides movies etc.

Even though I was quite worried about the war, etc., life was great at home, 18 years old, a car of my own, girls, etc., and I really enjoyed working on the farm. I worked in the gravel pit, helped Dad saw lumber with the portable saw mill he had made and the Buick straight eight power unit he had made from the motor from a big old Buick car. Also I had quite a firewood sawing business with the saw rig with the Dodge motor. I really enjoyed it. In those days before chain saws usually the farmer would haul pole wood into a big pile, then I would come with the saw rig and he would have three or four more men to help lift the poles up to the saw and I would saw it into wood about 16" in length so it could be split and then burned in the kitchen range or heating stove. The idea was you should have your wood cut, sawed, split, and piled up about a year ahead so it could dry. Whenever I sawed they gave us dinner or lunch, so it was great food, and fun to work with men when I was really only a kid. So much for that.

Another thing that was great in those days was roller skating to music with different types of couples only or couples of twos progressive. This was where each line when they blew the whistle the girl would move ahead to the next guy, and the girl behind would be your partner till they blew the whistle again. It was great for getting acquainted or getting a chance to skate with that beautiful girl you didn't know but hoped to!!! Then there were a lot of young people church activities or an occasional movie (this was before television); anyway, it was a great time. Some won't believe it, but I really was very shy, so I think I did more dreaming of dating than it actually happened. Ha?

But as the war got worse I just felt I had to go. So in the summer of 1944, I was 21 years old and deferred because of being needed on the farm. My deferment was running out so it either had to be renewed or I soon would be called. I didn't want another deferment, so I called the man on the draft board to tell him that, but before I got a chance to tell him why I called he must have thought I was calling to beg for another deferment so he gave a long speech of how hard it was for them to get enough guys to fill the quota. When he finally stopped talking long enough for me to tell him I didn't want to be deferred, his attitude really changed and I was put in 1A and was soon to be called. Dad didn't like it but felt I just had to go anyway. I may not have gotten deferred anyway.

Pretty soon I got notice to go to Milwaukee for my physical; that was a long bus ride with a whole bunch of guys. They put us in a hotel for the night, and our physicals were scheduled for the next day. Eight or so guys were all in one big room; I remember waking up because one of the guys was trying to jump out the window. We were up about ten floors there were two or three guys holding him back. He didn't jump, but I never forgot it.

The next day I passed my physical. I was in good health so even with a good physical I would have passed, but the talk was the Army needed men so bad that the physicals were pretty loose. Talk was that as you went through the line there was a doctor on both sides looking into your ears and if they couldn't see each other, you passed.

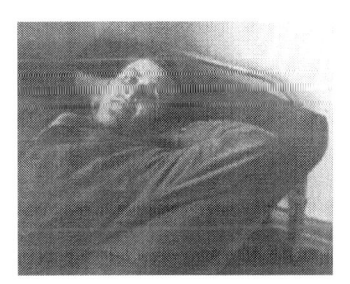

Carol, 1945

I could have gone home for a couple weeks, but I elected to go right in. So we were put on a train to Fort Sheridan, Illinois, to be outfitted for the infantry. We were there a few days getting our Army clothes, shoes etc. then we were off on the train for Camp Hood, Texas.

I remember it was an old sleeper car; it must have been from World War I. As a bashful country boy I think I was in a daze from the time we left Siren until we arrived in camp. Then I started to realize, I'm in the Army now; I'm not behind the plow.

Infantry basic was supposed to be 17 weeks at that time, but because the war was so bad in Europe they were shorting the basic because they needed men. So we didn't really know how long we would be there. They really worked us hard, long days,

Boarding the ship to go overseas.

40 and 8 boxcar.

Carol, Germany, 1945.

Carol with his army buddies.

The necessary stop.

lots of calisthenics, marching, hiking, etc., out in the field training most of the time. As a farm boy I was in pretty good shape, so I handled it pretty well, but some city boys really found it rough. I can honestly say I enjoyed it, but it was hard. Often they got us up at about 4:00 am to march out six to ten miles to some training field all day, then march back to camp to get in between 10:00 and 11:00 pm, and probably the same the next day. For a while the talk was we would be shipped out with nine weeks of training, but I think we got twelve weeks.

Then we got what they call a delay enroute, so I got a few days at home and then to Fort Mead, Maryland to be outfitted for overseas for about a week. I guess it was because we were headed overseas that they let us go on pass every night as long as we were back in the morning. Fort Mead is about forty miles from Washington DC. We got to Fort Mead on a Saturday, Sunday my buddy and I took the train to Washington DC; it was a beautiful spring day. The cherry blossoms were out, we walked by the capital and the Washington Memorial and on to the Lincoln Memorial. There were some young people playing softball and they invited us to play with them. Then we went with them to their church young peoples meeting. I don't know much of what my buddy did after that, but I got acquainted with a girl from Ohio working in Washington. Anyway I ended up going to Washington DC every night until we left for Camp Shanks, New York, where we shipped out from. This girl and I corresponded some when I was overseas, but when the war ended, it seems her interest in me ended! I guess she was just doing her duty to keep the GI's happy. Ha.

Carol with Army buddy, 1946.

Another memory I have of this time is the very night before we were to get on a ship to go to war in the European Theater was when President Roosevelt died. It made for a little more of a sobering thought; even though it seemed we were winning the war, we really didn't know what the future held.

We were in Camp Shanks only a couple of days when we were loaded on a big troop transport with a lot of GI's. Going out past the Statue of Liberty was a feeling I will never forget, especially since at that time the war was really bad. It was a big convoy and the German subs were very busy, so we were on the alert for subs several times, but we finally landed first in South

Hampton, England and then on to La Harve, France where we unloaded. We had to walk about two miles to the train depot with full field pack, and we were out of shape from the long trip on the boat and being seasick, etc. And to make matters worse as we were nearing the end of the trip they announced they had extra Hershey Bars and you could buy all you wanted and I must have bought many pounds to add to the full field pack. Anyway it was about the toughest trip I ever made and then too many Hershey bars. I hated Hershey bars for about ten years after that. La Harve was really bombed out; it was our first sight of the destruction of war.

They loaded us on some boxcars from the First World War; they called them the 40 and 8's (forty men or eight horses). I don't know how many men we were per car but it was standing room only, nothing but a small empty box car. It was pulled or pushed by old steam locomotives that were all shot up so the steam was pouring out wherever. We were either standing still or moving slowly. I don't think we ever got over twenty miles per hour.

It took three days to get from La Harve to an Army camp just outside of Paris; about two hours driving time. There we were issued our rifles and more equipment. Then we boarded a train for Germany and the front, or so we thought. We really had very little briefing or knowledge of what was going on. So what a surprise it was as we crossed into Germany and everywhere the white flags were flying, Germany had surrendered, and the war with Germany was over. I ended up being sent to a U.S Prisoner of War Camp near the Rhine River that the U.S. took over from the Germans where a lot of the Jews were killed. This was quite an experience for me. We were sent there to guard prisoners and displaced people in a sixty acre complex with high fences.

There were all kinds of people in there waiting to be interrogated, then either turned loose or sent somewhere else. The conditions for them were terrible. It rained a lot and there was just a sea of mud and they didn't get enough to eat so a lot died every night and day and they were buried in a big trench dug by bulldozers and then covered up.

We were a bunch of green soldiers who had never seen anything like this. Up until we came, the guards were mostly old soldiers who really hated the

Carol, Germany, 1946.

Germans, so at night they would fake sleep or whatever and when and if someone crawled over the fence, they would shoot them. When we got there we were told by the orientation captain that there would be no prisoners outside the fence but dead ones and if we held somebody at gunpoint, he would be called out there and he would make us shoot them. So if you didn't want to kill anyone, you'd better do a good job of walking and guarding your post. We didn't want to kill anyone, so after that there was hardly anyone who ever got out or was shot. But I will always have flashbacks of my time there. I don't know how long we were there, but then we were sent to a training camp, it seems like it was northwest of Frankfurt, where we were supposed to be training to go to the Japanese front. It seemed like we were shooting up a lot of the extra ammunition left over, when the war ended.

Army Jeep.

We had one experience here where we were in a practice field battle with live ammunition, and our own artillery fell on us. So we had two killed and about ten shot up with scraps. We were about twenty-nine guys in one group; we had not dispersed the way we should have, but the Captain had finally decided we maybe were not where we were supposed to be. I could have told him that, but I was just a Private carrying the Battalion Radio, so I don't think he would have listened to me. It had been a cold morning, so I had a heavy wool army sweater on. I was getting sweaty carrying that radio, so when he decided to stop to figure things out, I decided to take the sweater off. So I went off down kind of a bank and took the radio off and I was just pulling my sweater off when artillery landed right on us. The concussion knocked me down, but I wasn't hurt. As I stood up to see what had happened, as I remember it everyone was down with scraps or concussion, except this one soldier who had been all through North Africa, Italy, and France, and one of the falling down pieces of scrap metal had gone right through his steel helmet, and when he hit the ground he was dead.

I could write pages more about this day and the many acts of heroism. There was one medic in particular who was all shot up, but he kept instructing the rest of us what to do to help the other wounded. What saved me that day was I was over the bank taking my sweater off, so it missed me.

There were many more memorable experiences here, but none like the one I just talked about. Then we were shipped down to some place to await shipment to the Western Front. We were supposed to get on a troop train for Marseilles, France and board a ship to go to the Mediterranean Suez Canal, etc., to get to the Japanese Theater. Then that day, they dropped the atom bomb and so the plans were changed and we didn't go.

So I got to be in the Army of Occupation in Germany. At first, we moved from one small town to another fairly often. I didn't like the way it was done. I was still Radio Man and just a Private, but I got to ride in a jeep with the Captain or Colonel, and we would go into a town and he would pick out houses for the troops to move into, then give the people a few hours to move out and told them what they could take with them. Then our troops would move in for a few weeks or so. I thought this was bad and really unnecessary, because we were equipped to live outside. The worst part was when we moved on, the GI's would ruin the furniture and house as much as they could. I thought this was terrible but I couldn't do anything about it.

After some time our battalion got to take over security in Heidelberg, because the University of Heidelberg was where doctors from all over the world studied. So it was never bombed. It is a beautiful little city on the Neckar River that runs into the Rhine. There are beautiful old castles on the hills or mountains overlooking the city. At first we had too many places to guard with too few soldiers, but as they got things checked out we gradually needed guards in less places, so the job got easier. I was made a Corporal when we moved into Heidelberg, and because so many soldiers who had been in Europe a long time were gone, there got to be a real shortage of non-commissioned officers. So it wasn't long before I was a Sergeant; at the end of the war the military was not very strict. So if you just did your job, it was pretty easy.

Heidelberg Ferry, 1946.

I had a vacation of a lifetime for a few months in Heidelberg. There were quite a number of American GI's wives who were beautiful and well dressed, but the behavior of the Americans GI's was so bad so much of the time that they had to wear arm bands to show they were Americans, so the GI's would leave them alone. Then there were a lot of beautiful German girls whose main ambition was to dress like American girls, in hopes of getting a good GI boyfriend who might take them back to the States, and the GI's helped get these girls clothes, too. Some of these girls were not good, but many of them were very good. I know because I got to know a few.

The Army hired some German girls who could speak English and had experience in office work. In Battalion Headquarters where one of my buddies was clerk, there was a German girl working that I got acquainted with. She was a Christian and a really nice girl. In Heidelberg there was a serviceman's Christian league that I went to some. It was open to anyone who wanted to come including Germans. Anyway, because we had become acquainted in the Battalion office where she worked, she wanted to go to the serviceman's Christian league and asked me to walk with her because it was not too safe for good looking girls to be on the streets unless they had arm bands to tell that they were Americans or were accompanied by a GI. It was a mile or more from where she lived to where the meeting was. I walked with her there a few times, so we got acquainted. She was a very nice, good girl but to her I was a friend and protector she could trust. This was well and good but I guess I was thinking more like a girlfriend. We did remain just friends.

Then there was a beautiful young Hungarian girl who also came with her parents to this Bible study. We got acquainted, and she was studying to learn to speak English better, so I would go to their home to help her with her English lessons. It was also very interesting to hear them tell of their life because of the war, Hitler etc. To get to the English lessons, she and I would sit side by side to study English, very exciting! Except for one thing: her Dad would sit on the other side of her and her mother on the other side of me. There was no chance to do anything but study English, ha. I don't know how long this went on, but I was getting interested in Number Three, so this Hungarian girl faded out of the picture, but she was a beautiful, good girl, and I never forgot this experience.

Number Three was Hildy; she was just 17 and very pretty. She was the youngest of three girls whose parents owned or had owned the house that our battalion headquarters were in, but they had been forced out and were living in two or three rooms in a house close by; that was before we came into that outfit and Heidelberg.

Friend in Germany, 1946.

I don't know why, but usually when the Army moves in, the ones who pick out the places usually are not the ones that stay there. I think this is the way it was here. Anyway, it seemed like the brass (Captain, Sergeant), and the whole outfit felt sorry for those girls for getting forced out of their home, because they were really beautiful, nice girls. It seemed they got to be the sweethearts of our whole outfit, especially Hildy. She had the personality and beauty that would win anybody. So I don't know how it happened that I, a shy northern Wisconsin kid, got to be her boyfriend. For a while it was kind of secretive that we were special friends.

I have said and thought many times that winter, spring and summer of 1946 was the greatest vacation and best time I ever had. The Army was really loose and easy at that time. Not too much to do, and not enough discipline. Our outfit was responsible for security in Heidelberg, but it was a pretty peaceful, beautiful city, because of the medical University. It was never bombed, so there was no war damage. I think the bad behavior of our own GI's gave us more trouble than the Germans, because so many of the soldiers who had a lot of time in the war were being sent home, there was shortage of non-commissioned officers, sergeants, corporals etc. So I made Corporal, then soon Sergeant.

Since our security responsibility was quite easy, my Army job gave me a lot of free time. I would be sergeant of the guard every two or three days. If my memory is right, I think the sergeant of the guard was on a 12 hour shift. It was my responsibility to wake the guys for whatever length of shift they were on, two, three or four hours, and get them all in the truck with a driver, bring them to their post, and pick up the guard they were relieving. In between the change of guard it was my responsibility to be in the company office to answer the phone or take care of any problems. Another job was to go, or get someone else to go, to the Red Cross and pick up donuts. So we almost always had donuts and coffee available for the guards coming or going.

This was my job for about one 12 hour shift every three days or so, other than that we were supposed to be responsible for our part of the quarters until noon daily. From noon on, the day usually was mine to do whatever I decided

Carol with a group of Red Cross people.

Carol, 1945.

to do. In that time we had no formations marching or calisthenics, so it was pretty soft, but because so many guys had gone home, there was a shortage of specialized people like for communicator, etc. So if you opened your mouth that you knew anything about the problem you probably got the job to fix it. So I did get some jobs more than others just because I was dumb enough to try, but this was not often. So for the next part from noon every day was ours to do whatever we decided to do.

You noticed I said we: this was Hildy and I. I don't know for sure what the arrangements were, but our mess sergeant always had some food for Hildy to pick up at noon for her and her family. Two other guys and I were on the third floor of this building we were in, but there was a good view down the street the way she would come from. So I would watch for her and then I would rush down three flights of stairs and into the basement where they did the cooking etc. She would come in a back door that I think was left unlocked just in time so she could come in to get food for her family.

We found a secret place that it seemed no one knew about, and we would decide what to do in the afternoon. Then I would meet her at whatever time we decided. This was really a beautiful and romantic time with a beautiful young lady, in a beautiful setting. In my mind, Heidelberg is one of the most beautiful places in the world. It is about ten miles from Frankfurt on the Neckar River which flows into the Rhine about 30 miles from Heidelberg.

Up the river about forty miles from Heidelberg is Neckergomund, another picturesque town. The last couple of months before starting on the homeward stretch, I was stationed there. Heidelberg, which lays in the Neckar River Valley on the one side, was most of the city, then a bridge to the other side was North Heidelberg which also was quite a small city. This was where we were stationed, but most of our security duty was on the other side of the River. The last street along the river had houses on one side. On the other side was a quite wide strip of green, grassy area and then the river. It was a beautiful area

Postcard from Heidelberg

59

THE STARS AND STRIPES — Germany Edition
Daily Newspaper of U.S. Armed Forces in the European Theater of Operations

The Stars and Stripes was the weekly newspaper for the G.I.'s.

where on a nice day there would be a lot of people relaxing and laying and playing in the sun. It was a beautiful setting just across the road from the battalion headquarters house.

So Hildy and I would often spend time there, or walk across the river and up to the old castle. It was really picturesque and beautiful; it was also beautiful walking and sightseeing on the north side of the river. Another thing we did, with her knowledge of the area, was walk out the way there were orchards, truck gardens and farms. The farmers were not allowed to sell their produce yet, and still it was going to waste. So she would have a cloth bag to put fruit and vegetables in, and when no one was looking she would pick some into her bag. So when we got home she had food along. I guess it was stealing (or was it). I think sometimes we were seen doing it but for one thing it was going to waste otherwise. The other thing was that the Germans had respect or fear of an American soldier, so maybe they shut their eyes to it.

Occasionally GI's would sponsor get-together dances, etc., and Hildy would be (at least in my eyes) the most beautiful girl there. She loved to dance, but I didn't dance, so she danced with a lot of the guys. I just watched, but between the dances she always came back to our table. It made me the envy of a lot of the guys. So you can see why I had a beautiful winter, spring, and summer, 1946 until I came home in September. I guess we were in love, but believe me I never had sex with Hildy. This is the truth (not like Clinton). The reason was that we both believed this was for marriage.

I mention this no sex part because it is so seemingly OK, but it shouldn't be. I believe this is one of the main reasons for so many divorces and broken families. So my hope would be that younger people that might read this would consider this thought.

Anyway, to get back to

Carol by Cafe Timberline.

60

Carol and Army Buddies.

Germany, the Army, and Hildy. She was sure we were made for each other, etc., and hoped to be able to come home with me (or after me) and we would get married and live happily ever after. It was a beautiful dream, and I did really care about her, but I wasn't sure she realized what it would be like to come to northern Wisconsin to marry and live with a country boy just home from the service with hardly any money, just trying to make a life, as they say now. She did know a lot about hard times, working for food and clothes and what they had to do, even as kids, with Hitler gradually losing the war. It became harder and harder on everyone and even as kids they were being taught to fight and march, etc. So when the war ended and things got a little better, I'm sure that spring and summer we had together in Heidelberg was almost like heaven on earth for her too, but to get her to understand what it would be like to be the wife of a poor boy in northern Wisconsin was quite impossible. I cared so much for her that most of me said go for it! I didn't write home about it to anyone except my sister Dorothy. I sort of was asking her for advice; she didn't say yes or no, just that we should be sure.

It got closer and closer to the time to go home and it would have been impossible for her to come with me. So we decided we would write often and whatever would be would be.

Those of us going home were sent to a coming in and going out camp for two or three weeks. This was a hard place for me because I was a Sergeant and I was expected to be able to handle a platoon of men, march, give close order drill, etc. I never was any good at marching, let alone giving the commands, because in Heidelberg we hardly ever had a formation. The ones we had to march, drill, etc. were the green, incoming boys. Mostly they could march better then me. It didn't take long to see someone pretty good, so I would turn the platoon over to him if I saw any brass coming around to see how we were doing.

Another memory I have of that camp is: one weekend three or four of

Carol bossing.

Carol, August 5, 1945.

us got passes and hitchhiked to Heidelberg. The Germans would give you a ride maybe, but we didn't have very good luck so we did a lot of walking and I remember we rode on a wagon pulled by a tractor for many miles. We did get to Heidelberg and I did get to see Hilda. It was very exciting; this was the last time I saw her, and we kissed goodbye. I did talk to her on the phone in 1973 when Irene and I took a trip over there when Arlen was over there in the Army. He went to see her several times, he said she was just as pretty as ever. He didn't like it that she treated him like she was his aunt or mother or something. Ha!

I don't remember how we got back to the camp when we hitchhiked from to Heidelberg, but we did. We soon were sent by train up to Bremerhaven, where we were for a few days and then we got on a victory ship (they held about 1,500 soldiers). It was beautiful weather coming home. We came down the English Channel, so we came right by the white cliffs of Dover. This was a beautiful sight. I think it was about ten days until we landed in New York. It was full moon time and the nights were just beautiful. One of the buddies I was with in Heidelberg was on this ship too, so we had a beautiful time laying on the deck in the moonlight remembering about our days over there, especially in Heidelberg. I got a little seasick for a day or two, but not bad.

As we were coming into New York we watched as the statue of Liberty came into view; it got closer and we sailed right by it, the same as we did going out. That is really a great experience.

White Cliffs of Dover.

I think it was Camp Kilmer, New Jersey we went to for three or four days and we got a pass to New York City. My buddy had relation on Long Island, where we stayed overnight. We got mixed up going the wrong way on the subway, but we finally got there. We did spend a little time in the red light district where they seem to take the homecoming soldiers, but I didn't think too much of it. Then we were sent on to Fort Sheridan, Illinois (near Chicago) where I was discharged from, then on to St. Paul and from there I got on the train to Frederic and home. Oh Boy!!

Chapter Seven: Coming Home and Getting Started

I was excited, but when the train stopped in Frederic there was nobody there to meet me. I guess they knew I was coming soon but didn't know exactly when. Anyway, I got a ride with a lady hauling newspapers somewhere out to Four Corners, where my sister Arlene lived then, and she brought me home. I was a little disappointed because they were eating supper. I don't think Daddy was home; only a couple of my sisters and brothers came out to welcome me home. I thought they sure didn't miss me much!! Oh well, I was still glad to be home. I fixed up a room in the upstairs of the old house that wasn't being used, and that was my room for now.

Grantsburg Train Station.

The day I arrived home I was hoping and expecting there would be some mail from Hildy, but there wasn't any. These were rather hard times for me because I didn't know she wouldn't write to me, I wrote to her and just kept looking for mail. I guess after two or three months I about gave up.

What happened was that we had an agreement with another soldier to send her letters to me and I send my letters to him to give to her because the Army mail was much faster. Anyway, he wasn't honest with her because he was trying to win her, so he took her letters to me and said he sent them but he didn't, and the same with my letters to her. This went on until sometime during the summer of 1947, she found out what he was doing. So in about August of 1947 here comes a letter from her to me, but I was already married to Ardelle. Our mail usually came around noon and I didn't come from work until evening, so Ardelle had gotten our mail and found this letter from Hildy in Germany. I don't remember for sure, but I think she had opened it and read it. She didn't tell me right away but she was very quiet, and I knew something must be wrong.

She finally showed it to me and there were some very tense moments with me trying to explain. I hadn't told her about this at all for a couple of reasons. Number one, I thought because I didn't get any letters Hildy had dropped me, so why tell her about it. Number two, Ardelle was a beautiful, wonderful young girl and I had fallen madly in love with her, so I didn't want to talk to her about any former love affairs. So I had a problem but I did tell her all about it. I did manage to get her to believe it wasn't going to change our lives together and I talked her into writing to Hildy and telling her about us. She did, and Hildy wrote back and they got to be friends and wrote each other from then on.

So now to get back to when I had just got out of the Army. I always loved machinery, especially saw mills and the power to run them. To this day I still am not sure which I loved the most (aside from girls, ha), horses or machinery. In my teen years in the 1930's when Daddy taught me and then trusted me to cut hay, cultivate, plow, etc., it was really great and then when I could drive the horses on the grain binder, and corn binder.

It is like a great dream to think back on the sawmill days before I was in the Army. I was anxious to do some of these things. The Buick power unit was a little tired and had some problems such as overheating, etc. and I kind of wanted a big tractor that I could pull the sawmill or thresher machine or whatever, besides using it for belt power. In case some of you don't know what belt power is, even in the 40's and 50's it still was used on sawmills, thresher machines, etc. It was a flat belt six to ten inches wide, and sixty to one hundred fifty feet long, that would run on a flat pulley on the tractor or power unit to a flat pulley on whatever machine you needed to use. But with a tractor that you could move with its own power, it was much easier to line the belt up so it would stay on, and also to tighten it up so it wouldn't slip.

Carol filing the big lumber saw, a job he had to do at least 4 times a day, 6 days a week, for at least 15 years.

Anyway, I was looking for a big tractor and then a man between home and Grantsburg that had a tractor and threshing machine with a good run of customers who because of health wanted to sell. This was within a month from when I got discharged. It was late August or early September of 1946. Most

Sawmill.

of the grain threshing was done but this machine had all the attachments for threshing grass seed. Grass seed threshing (mostly clover and alfalfa) was done in the fall after the grain and there weren't many machines that could do it. So if you had a machine that could do it, you probably ended up covering a lot bigger territory than for grain threshing. I had saved a little when in the Army, so I used this and borrowed the rest, and I never have been completely out of debt since. Ha!

Within just a few weeks of being discharged from the Army, here I was the thresher man and enjoying it. It is a dusty, dirty job but I loved it, partly because Daddy and a couple of neighbor boys had a sawmill and thresher machine, and my Grandpa Okerstrom did a lot of the threshing in the same area that I now had in the late 1800's, and my customers would tell me about my Grandpa when he threshed. These of course were the older men who probably were young or kids when the Grandpa I never knew did the threshing and lumber sawing, etc.

So I was happy to be home and doing work, but every day I was hoping for a letter and it didn't come. I think I was in love with that girl, so it was kind of hard, but I did have mixed feelings because I was not sure I would be able to keep her happy in my situation and what I could offer. It would have been a big change from her life over there.

Anyway, I guess I was starting to look at the girls around home. One of the hometown girls was the most faithful in writing to me when I was in the service.

Hauling sand lift before blacktopping.

She was a nice girl; I'm not sure what she had in mind, but I never really thought of her as anything but a friend and good writer to a lonesome country boy in the army. She was a neighbor girl from our church. A lot of girls at that time after high school went to the Cities, Minneapolis or St. Paul, for work or college or both, because there was not much work for a young lady around here. I am not sure how it came about, but she and my first wife, Ardelle, ended up rooming together, they were good friends and so she brought her home for the weekend. Possibly because this soldier she had been writing to had just come home.

There was a young people's meeting at this girl's home that night. So I met old friends and especially my letter writer friend and, even more special, this roommate of hers, Ardelle. She was a beautiful young lady (18 years old; I was 23) I was immediately attracted to her but I don't know if anything would have come of it except for tires. Just after the war ended it was really hard to find a car to buy and tires were even harder to get. I had found and bought a 1935 Ford Coupe, but the tires were bad. It was a nice little car for $500.00, which was probably more than it cost new. In the 1930's you could buy a brand

Ardelle.

new car for around $400.00, but that money was probably harder to come by than the $20,000.00 or so to buy a new one now.

After lunch that evening we talked about this and that, and we talked about that I needed tires for my car. At that time, at some places where you worked that sold tires you could get a tire allotment for your car or a friend's car. Ardelle (my future wife) worked at Montgomery Wards and they sold tires. She didn't have a car but had a tire allotment so she could buy four tires. We talked about this but I didn't know if I dared to ask her if she could or would get me tires.

I will always remember that night. I had gone down to my car and Ardelle & Mabel were standing on the porch to say goodbye and suddenly Ardelle called out, would you really want me to get you some tires? And that's how it all started! She did get me tires. She and Mabel lived only three or four blocks from the big Wards store and she rolled those tires one at a time from the store home, and I got them from there.

Ad for Peterson Lumber.

From there our romance went like wildfire. I teased her about this tire deal for all our years together. This was late August, and by November or early December I had bought her an engagement ring. Her folks were not too happy about it, but I guess we were determined. Ardelle's folks were from Cambridge, Minnesota, but they had become friends with some people from Roseau, Minnesota that had moved to Los Angeles and they invited Ardelle's folks to come out there for the winter. That was great except their young beautiful daughter had just gotten engaged to a northern Wisconsin jackpine savage. Ha.

They did talk her into or ordered her to come to California too, hoping they could break us up, but it didn't work. It was a winter I will never forget. We were still threshing grass seed when she took the train to California. Wade Brask was working with me and I had gotten a lot bigger territory to cover and the weather was not cooperating, so we didn't get done and pulled home until my birthday January 29, 1947. Then I moved Daddy's sawmill and my big tractor to a big job about fifteen miles from home. I "bached" it in an old abandoned house and came home most weekends, but I got a letter almost every day and had to write one almost every day so we kept our love going. We had wedding plans for June of 1947. Pretty exciting.

It was a very special day when she came home the early part of March by train from Los Angeles to Minneapolis. Her folks were coming with her, so her brother and sister-in-law were meeting them. I had some problems because I had sold my 1935 Coupe and was waiting for a really nice 1939 Chevy five passenger Coupe, but right then I only had a 1932 Chevy Coupe I had bought from a junk dealer and fixed up and put a box on to make it sort of a pick-up for the sawmill job: hauling tools, gas, oil, etc. It was not a very nice machine to pick up your bride to be and meet her folks and family, but we made it and started from

Ardelle and Carol with the 1935 Ford Coupe.

that train depot.

We got only a couple miles and that jalopy stopped and I couldn't get it going. Finally, I found out it was out of gas. I had filled it up with gas but I didn't know there was a big dent in the gas tank so it only held about eight gallons of gas and here she was sitting in there like a beautiful flower in a weed patch afraid to touch anything. What a deal, we were supposed to go to her brother's place for a late breakfast, but by now she was not too happy with me or with the situation. So we went and rented a car for the rest of the weekend.

All went well until Sunday afternoon and I had to take the rented car back and pick up the old jalopy and take her home to Cambridge and then back to Wisconsin. We were going up Highway 65 north towards Cambridge at a good speed and all of a sudden there was a clattering and banging. I didn't know what had happened; I got it stopped and discovered the front bumper had broken on one end and it was dragging on the pavement. Luckily, I had a piece of rope in the box so I tied it up so it didn't drag, and away we went. When we got to Cambridge to her folk's house, her sister and brother-in-law were supposed to come and her folks weren't home yet. We didn't want them to see the jalopy so we parked it out in back, but low and behold when they came they came in the back way, so they saw it anyway.

What a time, but she never got upset like she might have. We kidded and teased about this off and on for all of our years together. For the life of me, I will never understand everything about why we were getting married in Trade Lake Church instead of her home church in Cambridge, Minnesota. I think maybe there were several reasons. First of all, I don't think her parents thought I was good enough for their daughter (I guess they really maybe were right), but that wasn't going to stop us from

Carol and Ardelle, about 1947. Our 1952 Ford, first car we bought new.

getting married in Trade Lake Church. Cambridge in that era had a sort of superior attitude. If you were from Cambridge you were just a little above the rest of the world, and at that time I'm not sure that her folks could afford a proper Cambridge wedding. Also, I suppose they were afraid she was pregnant. We fooled anybody who worried about this because our first child, Susan, wasn't born until almost a year after we were married.

Mid 1930's, after Bernard Richter came home from serving in the Marines. L-R: Dorothy holding Alice, Pete Erickson, Gladys looking down at Bobby, Florence In front of Arlene, Sibyl In front of Bernard, Pearl in front of Carol.

Sister Dorothy at her wedding to
Harold Baker.

Ardelle with sister Bernice,
1958.

Carol with Dorothy and Harold
Baker by 1935 Coupe.

Sister Pearl in the 1940's.

Sister Arlene at her wedding
to Clarence Lee.

Chapter Eight: Married Life

We decided to get married in my church in Trade Lake. We had a beautiful wedding, but not so expensive, if I remember right. Ardelle and I paid for it, with the help of my family, relatives and friends. She came from California around May first, and the wedding was set for early June. So she was a busy girl. She sewed her own wedding dress and it was beautiful. For an 18 year old she really could sew. After we were married she sewed almost all of her own clothes and for our kids and more wedding dresses.

All the wedding plans, decorating etc. kept her very busy that month. My cousin Mavis really helped her a lot. I don't remember or think I was much help mostly because how can a Jack Pine savage help plan a wedding? I was busy getting my saw milling done so I could take a couple of weeks off for our honeymoon. I moved the sawmill up to Clarence and Arlene Lee's my sister and brother-in-law, since I had a job to saw for them as soon as we got back from our honeymoon.

Carol and Ardelle on their wedding day.

The wedding went very well, and so we were off on our honeymoon. We stayed the first night at Stillwater, Minnesota. This was an elegant place and she really wanted to stay there. What a night (one we had been waiting for), then off towards Chicago and into Michigan. We stayed the second night near Jackson, Michigan. The next night we went to Niagara Falls; that is a place like no other and we really enjoyed it and of course each other. Then on to Buffalo, New York and then down to Cleveland, Ohio and on to Chicago where we stayed one night in a high rise overlooking Lake Michigan, then back home to start our life together.

I am now 78 years old and when I think of teens to twenty year old people today, I think of them as kids, and yet I think we really felt grown up. I do think young people in those days did mature younger. I guess that depends on each individual and the environment they grow up in.

My reason for writing this was to show the changes from then until now and it seems the best way to do this is telling the experiences of my own life. Those first 25 years or so that I have written about so far are perhaps the biggest changes. From the days of perhaps more horses in town than cars, and then the great changes in cars as the years went by. Also the changes in farming: from using mostly horses to tractors, and the unbelievable progress in tractors and farm equipment and machinery of every kind.

Now, to get back to Ardelle and I starting our life together. We had rented a house just across from my folks before the wedding and had bought some furniture so we were partially ready to move in when we got home. We got organized somewhat in our rented home, but then I had to do that lumber sawing job at Clarence and Arlene's, so we stayed there during the week and slept on the floor on their porch. What a way to treat a new bride, but she seemed to love it. After a few weeks, that job was done and we moved the mill to a job close to home. I had one hired man (Philip), and my brother who was 13 years old worked part time for me. So it went pretty well, they helped us a lot. Bobby was kind of a jack-of-all-trades (like my Dad), and he needed work, so I gave him all the work I could. As I said he did need the work, so he also did need to get paid. But sometimes when I wasn't home it seemed he got in a lot of hours for what he got done. I was a hard worker, and was sometimes called a slave driver. So sometimes this thing called patience, which neither he or I had too much of almost would cause a blow up, but in the long haul them moving close to us was a blessing.

Clarence and Arlene's house where we slept on the floor on the porch.

Anyway things were going great and then one day that letter came from Germany, and if Ardelle hadn't been the wonderful girl she was, it might have messed up everything. But Hildy seemed to understand, and so she and Ardelle got to be pen pals. So it really didn't hurt our marriage. Things were going along great.

Then something happened that I think changed our life. There was an ad in the Wisconsin Farmer magazine that Daddy saw and told me about. It was about a highly portable saw mill you could set up and be sawing lumber in about one half hour average set up time for Daddy's mill (a day to one and half days). It was coming down by Amery, about 40 miles away. It was called

Jackson Lumber Harvester.

a Jackson Lumber Harvester, the builder was Clint Jackson, and it was one of his brothers Homer who came up with it that day. I got there about the same time he did and there wasn't hardly anyone else around yet. So I ended up helping him set it up and turned logs for him when he was sawing. It was quite the machine and I got really interested. Homer, the guy who brought the mill up there and operated it, was something else. He was a great big strong guy with a loud voice, but I thought not too many brains.

I got excited about getting a mill like it. The big problem was that it cost about $4,000.00 for just the mill; that would compare with about $40,000.00 today. I think Daddy was sorry he encouraged me to go down and see it, because he didn't think there was enough timber left around here to make enough work for a mill that cost that much. My dad was seldom wrong on anything, but I think he was this time, for three main reasons. Number 1: there was more timber and growing timber than he realized. Number 2: it was a time when lumberyards were high priced for the farmers. So if they needed to build new barns, sheds, etc., and had some lumber they would cut logs and we would come in and saw it into lumber for them so they could afford to build. We also sawed for a lot of houses. Number 3: I don't think he realized how fast we could saw, and with more accuracy than most mills.

I really wanted to get that new mill and felt it was the right thing to do. If Dad would have signed with me I think I could have bought it, but he was already hard up and besides, he didn't think it was a good thing. So what now???

One of my friends from church, Sunday school, 4-H, etc., who was also newly married was going to college in St. Paul, but he wasn't very sure that was what he wanted to do. They were visiting us on a Sunday afternoon and I was telling him about this highly portable sawmill, Jackson Lumber Harvester, and they really got interested in it too. So what happened was, he quit college, they moved home, rented a house and we went into partnership. This was the start of Peterson-Nord that

Jackson Lumber Harvester.

went for years. I think we did a good job and were honest, so we got a good reputation and were soon very busy. For several years we always had a list of fifteen to thirty jobs, big and small, waiting for us.

Francis Nord was really something else, very intelligent, the best partner a guy could have. He was big, strong, ambitious, hard working, honest and a Christian. We worked very well together. Anyway, we got that new Jackson Lumber Harvester Saw Mill. For the first few months we used my big Allis-Chalmers Rummley for power. We needed an edger; if you don't know what an edger is, it's a separate machine to take the bark edges off boards that come off the head saw before the log is all square. You can do it on the big saw but this is slow. So we wanted an edger.

Carol with his tractor, his pride and joy, in about 1948.

We bought a used edger, and mounted it on a two-wheel trailer that we built. Then we made a power unit out of 1932 4-cycle Plymouth car engine, made a governor for it and mounted it above the edger with a v-belt drive down to the edger. Then we were ready to make lumber. Wow!!! This machine created quite an excitement wherever we went because of fast set up. Big production, quality lumber compared to most mills in the area. We could saw enough lumber for a house or barn in a couple of days, if we had good logs.

We were very busy, but we found we needed more horsepower and something faster moving on the road than the tractor. And when harvest time came, as busy as the sawmill was, we really needed to run both at the same time, and we had to have the tractor for threshing. We had made a little money, so we could make a down payment. So we bought a GMC Diesel Power unit on payments. We bought a 1935 Ford truck and mounted the power unit on it, and mounted the edger on the side with a v belt drive from the diesel. The mill was powered with a wide flat belt from the diesel. So when we'd get the mill leveled up and line the truck with the power unit on it,

Jackson Lumber Harvester

so the belt was lined, the edger was on the truck, so in minutes we were sawing lumber.

Anyway to get back to my life with Ardelle; we were having a great life together. But it kept us hopping. The people we were renting from sold the place so we had to move. We moved to the Village of Trade Lake, about two and a half miles away. The man that owned that house was a little old man that was our neighbor for years, a good neighbor but he could be stubborn. We rented the downstairs, and he lived upstairs. The problem was, there was no water upstairs, so he had to come down for water. He wouldn't let us lock the door, so we never knew when he would come in. He believed because it was his house he could come in whenever he wanted to without knocking. The stairs coming down came into the entryway, so he could come into our place or go outside. So if we heard him coming down the steps we had to either be ready or hide. Ha.

Then one day Ardelle told me she thought she was pregnant, and the doctor confirmed it. We were going to be parents!! The due date was sometime in May or early June. Health-wise, she was doing very well. Susan was born May 8th 1948. She was a healthy, happy baby, but it was quite the experience for Ardelle. It took hours and Ardelle was in a lot of pain, and because she hurt, I hurt right along with her. That was some day! But we now had a family, a beautiful little girl.

In those days there were no parenting classes, etc., so what you knew was just from helpful parents and friends and a little from the doctor and some good nurses. In those days they would keep the mother and baby in the hospital for about a week. One thing that is so different from then until now was the bill. Would you believe $36.00 for the total bill, hospital stay, doctor, everything. Of course, $36.00 then was probably more like $1,000.00 or more now.

Ardelle and Carol with Susan, 1948.

A comparison of from then until now was wages. I was hiring some help before there was a wage law. I had an older man who worked for me part time who believed nobody was worth over $.50 an hour. Most of the help I hired I was paying $.90 or $1.00 hour, but he wouldn't take more than $.50. Then the first minimum wage law was passed at $.90 hour. So, being an honest, law abiding Christian, he said okay I'll take it, but he said, I'll give $.40 an hour of it to my church. That was also at the time when Social Security was started. So as an employer I had to withhold and pay in to Social Security and withholding income tax.

Now to get back to Ardelle, our daughter Susan, and that believe it or not I was a father. It was going really well, but here I must bring another person into the story, Sibyl Richter. Her husband, Hardy Richter was my stepmother's brother. Hardy was a great guy. They got married just before he went in the Army in World War II. He served in the South Pacific, was wounded a couple times, but lived. Finally, when the war was over he came home. They bought a farm right next to his folks, Grandpa and Grandma Richter. They had a few cows, a team of horses, pigs, and chickens. This was in the fall of 1948. They were trying to farm but it didn't seem to be going very well. The war was hard on Hardy. He wasn't the same fun, good guy that he was before the war. Hardy's brother Bob had rigged up a sawmill and was sawing a few miles from home. He had an accident and broke his leg so he couldn't work. So Hardy was sawing for him. Then a terrible thing happened, a board fell into the head saw, was thrown back like a bullet and hit Hardy in the head and killed him. That was a really sad day. I was sawing lumber that day too, and when I came home Ardelle told me what had happened. This was really a shock for everybody.

This left Sibyl alone, and she was one of the most caring persons I ever knew. She sold out the livestock, machinery, etc. They had bought the farm from a neighbor, so he bought it back. So she lived here and there, mostly with Hardy's brother, Dick. Because I guess she was somewhat available, she

Sibyl in the 1980's.

got started staying with couples that were expecting babies. From before the baby came and for a while after. So she came and stayed with us before Susan was born and for a while after, same thing when Kathy came along, and then Arlen, and then Dwight.

Susan was born in 1948. It must have been 1949 when we bought our first house of our own, right in the Village of Trade Lake. We bought it from Fred Gustafson who had a store right across the road from the house. Gustafson's Store had been a part of Trade Lake since the early 1900's. It was pretty big and he sold everything, groceries, shoes, clothes, hardware, farm machinery, gas, and oil.

Upstairs in the store was a good size dance floor, about 40' X 60' with a platform on one end for the band. Fred could really play the piano. My folks didn't believe in dancing so we never went there, but I remember once I was with Daddy in Trade Lake on a Saturday night when they were swinging it upstairs. At the time there were two taverns in Trade Lake. This was about in the early 1930's. Fred had closed the store in the early 1940's and moved to the house his folks had, and wanted to sell the house in Trade Lake.

It was and still is a pretty small house, kitchen, dining room, living room downstairs, and two bedrooms and bathroom upstairs. It did have running water if you could keep it from freezing up. It had a beautiful yard with evergreens, flowering crab trees, and flowers of different kinds. It was really a neat place. I got a GI loan and bought it for $1,600.00.

After a couple of years, I bought the old store for $200.00. I put a new roof on it. The bottom floor made a good work and lumber storage area. The upstairs we fixed up a little and used it for a place for the young people to play basketball or whatever. There was really a lot of fun had up there. I put a basement under about two thirds of the house, fixed it up quite a bit. When we bought what there was of Birchwood Beach in 1955, I sold the house in Trade Lake for $4,500.00.

In March of 1951, Kathy was born; now we had two beautiful little girls. In 1952 we bought our first brand new car, a 1952 Ford Tudor. This was quite an event for me because in the

Ardelle holding Kathy, Susan, on steps of house in Trade Lake.

1930's as I was growing up, I didn't feel deprived, but I never expected I would ever be able to buy a brand new car.

In 1953 we took a trip in that car, first down to Oklahoma to visit my army buddy Jack and his wife Velta Rae, then down to Arkansas and on down to Alabama, we went to Bellingrath Gardensby, Mobile. This was the most beautiful place and flowers that I had ever seen. Then we visited another army buddy, they were in truck gardening. It was interesting. I was in Germany with him and we came home together, as I mentioned before. After this visit we went on down to Florida to Disney World and many of the other places such as Cypress Gardens, Busch Gardens etc.

Then it was cherry blossom time in Washington D.C. I had been there just before I went overseas. It was so beautiful I wanted Ardelle to see it. So we drove up through the Carolinas and into the state of Virginia, but Ardelle wasn't feeling well by the time we got to Richmond, Virginia, so we decided we had better stop and get a motel and call a doctor. We asked the people at the motel about a doctor. They said at night the best chance was to call their family, a mostly retired and older family doctor. So they called him for us and in just a little bit he was there.

He said almost right away that he thought it was an appendix attack but because we had been driving all day he thought it could be just carsickness, so he made a prescription and said we should call him anytime of the night if she got worse. I said yeah, but what about the prescription? He said that's no problem. He said he would stay there with Ardelle and the girls while you go get it. What a guy!!! So I got the medicine and he went home, but the pain didn't let up so about 6 am I called him and he came right over.

At that point, he thought for sure it was her appendix, and should be operated on as soon as possible. He said the only place he felt that could happen was at the University Hospital Emergency Center. So he gave me directions to take her there. I said okay, but what about the girls, he said don't worry, I'll take them home with me; again, what a guy.

So not knowing what was going on or what to expect, we went down to the emergency part of the University Hospital about 6:45 am; I think it was a

Susan, Kathy, 1954.

Sunday morning. They must have had a lot of accidents that night, because there were police and ambulance sirens, and wounded and bloody people coming in. Despite that it seemed to be general chaos, they did get Ardelle into a bed, but nothing seemed to be happening for her. So I tried to find out and get it through their heads that we did have hospital insurance. Then pretty soon they moved her into a regular room way up on the seventh floor and a doctor came in and talked to us and they gave her something to ease the pain and by afternoon she was a little better. The doctor said he was sure she needed an appendix operation, but if we would fly home she could have it at home. To get a quick flight, she would have to fly from Washington DC, about 100 miles from Richmond. So I think they made the reservations on a flight to Minneapolis about four hours from then.

So Ardelle got released, and we were off to pick up Susan and Kathy at that old doctor's house. This is really the heart of the story because when we got there the girls were having such a good time they weren't even missing us. The doctor and his wife had a beautiful place and would you believe they had two grandchildren about the same age as ours with the same names, only the oldest was Kathy and the youngest was Susan, and the four were busy playing out in a big yard. Ardelle and I met the doctor's wife and visited a little, but we had to rush if we were going to make that plane in DC.

So I asked the doctor, "What do I owe you?" He said, "I get one dollar a house call if it's not too far, and it was two calls, so that's two dollars." I said, "But I owe for taking care of the girls." We were both standing close and I will never forget his arm across my shoulder as he said, "My boy, there are some things money don't buy." Boy, that's real southern hospitality. So I gave him the two dollars and we thanked them both. Ardelle got their name and address and we were off to Washington DC to make that flight.

I was still determined that Ardelle should see the cherry blossoms in DC. It seemed we had an extra half hour to the plane, so we did see cherry blossoms just from the car, but then I read the signs wrong or something because we almost missed the plane, but we made it. Kathy went with Ardelle on the plane and Susan and I took off in the car. This was before too many freeways. It was really a lot of hilly crooked roads in West Virginia and Ohio driving all night. We got to Illinois, but I was so tired I felt we had to get some rest so we stopped in a motel overnight. I had called Ardelle's sister and brother-in-law, so they met Ardelle and Kathy's plane and stayed with them until we got there the next day. Susan was good the whole time; we got to Minneapolis and picked Ardelle and Kathy up and went on to Frederic. We stopped at the hospital, and the doctor put her in the hospital and she didn't get home until after she had the appendix operation. In those days they kept you in the hospital a few

Susan, Kathy, 1954.

days after an operation.

That was a beautiful trip except after Ardelle got sick, but it all turned out well and we were very thankful. Sibyl stayed with us before and after Kathy was born too. All the while we were very busy sawing lumber, threshing, also hauling cattle to South St. Paul. In 1954, Ardelle was pregnant again. We were sawing over by Rush City, Minnesota on a big job. So I was gone for long days, but Sibyl was living with us. So if Ardelle had to go to the hospital, she could take her, and that's the way it happened. I will never forget that night I came home and stopped at Clifford Baldwin's store close to the house. I came in the store and Clifford said I hear you got a new hired man today. I guess I looked at him kind of dumb like, and he said don't you know Ardelle had a baby boy today. No, I didn't know, I had better get home and get to the hospital to see Ardelle and our son Arlen. I got up there and they were doing fine. It was a day to remember, December 9th 1954. Now we were a family of five.

L-R: My sisters Muriel and Alice, and my sister Arlene's children: Sharon, Rodney, and Wayne. Mid-1950's.

JACKSON LUMBER HARVESTER, INC.

MANUFACTURERS OF THE FAMOUS LUMBER HARVESTERS, TYMILS, AND TRAILER EDGERS

PHONE 585
BREWTON, ALA.
U.S.A.

CLINTON D. JACKSON, President
GOTHARD C. WALLER, Vice-Pres.
E. J. FUMERITE, Sec'y-Treasurer

April 12, 1949

Mr. Carrol Peterson
Peterson & Nord Lumber Harvester Service
Route #1
Frederic, Wisconsin

Dear Mr. Peterson:

      Your letter of April 8th arrived this morning just an hour after Mr. Jackson left for Wisconsin. In all liklihood he can give you a better picture of the values in having an edger through personal, or telephone conversation with you than I can by mail, so I am sending a copy of your letter and this one to him via Air Mail.

      Quite likely he will arrive in Mondovi Thursday or Friday and he will communicate with you be telephone, sometime between then and Sunday. If he has not reached you by Monday noon please call him at Mondovi, c/o the Morton Moe residence phone. And, if possible, please arrange with the telephone operator to take or make the call at a Frederic telephone as the last conversation with you over a rural connection was not very satisfactory.

      In the meantime, in order to expedite the transaction, I am sending the following information so you will be able to reach an early decision.

      The enclosed circular lists the various types of Miner Edgers and special parts such as Hinged Side Rail, etc. You will notice that there was a raise in price of Miner Edgers effective December 15, 1948 of 12½ %. Present prices are as follows:

    MINER EDGER -- F.O.B. Meridian, Miss. $423.00
        (02-26" is now called a 4-26")
        Includes 2 14" Inserted Tooth saws, and
        has SKF Ball Bearing Mandrel

    JACKSON-MINER TRAILER EDGER   564.16
        Includes: Miner Edger (4-26"), Axle,
        Springs, Sub Base, Tow Bar, Jack, Crank
        (Less Tires and Tubes)

JACKSON LUMBER HARVESTING EQUIPMENT MAKES SELECTIVE CUTTING PRACTICAL
"Lumber Harvester" Copyrighted U. S. A. and Foreign Countries

Sales Letter received 1949 from Jackson Lumber Harvester. Page 1

2....Mr. Carol Peterson

    JACKSON-MINER TRAILER EDGER WITH VF-4 ENGINE $978.80
        Includes: Miner Edger (4-26"), Axle,
        Springs, Sub Base, Tow Bar, Crank,
        Engine Base, 4-Cylinder VF-4 Wisconsin
        Air-Cooled Engine Installed
        (Less Tires and Tubes)

        This engine is suitable for custom service

    JACKSON-MINER TRAILER EDGER WITH VP-4 ENGINE $1051.80

        Includes: Same as above excepting it has
        a VP-4 engine which is more suitable for
        commercial use.

    The Miner Edger can be shipped within 10 days of receipt of the order; the mounted edgers can be shipped within 10 to 20 days. Prices are F.O.B. Brewton.

    We are pleased that you have informed us that you have sold your first Jackson Lumber Harvester to Mr. Otto Gustafson of Hinckley, Minn. We desire to be of service to owners of our equipment, and I am writing him to day, and enclosing information which may be of value to him in getting started in that territory. I am assuming that you have passed along an Operator's Manual to him. We will put him on the list for monthly shipments of bits starting May 1.

    We recommend a "good grade" of bearing grease for the mandrel bearings, and suggest that you follow the Operator's Manual carefully in applying it. We have in stock Keystone #44 which costs you 40¢ per lb. in 7-lb. tins, f.o.b. Brewton. You will be able to learn from charts in your local distributor's shop what other brands of grease are similar to Keystone if you wish to buy it locally.

    Thank you for your remittance in payment of saw bits.

    If you are unable to get in touch with Mr. Jackson or wish to take immediate action before talking with him we will be glad to take your order by phone or wire. If so please verify the order by letter with 10% down payment, balance to be paid SDBL.

    HOW'S THAT BABY GETTING ALONG?

                Sincerely yours,

                Maurice Aase
                Director of Public Relations

MA:s
Enc. - 2

Sales Letter received 1949 from Jackson Lumber Harvester. Page 2

Sales Letter received 1949 from Jackson Lumber Harvester. Page 3

Greater Lumber Profits for You
with the Jackson-mounted
MINER EDGER
TRAILER-TYPE

**Saves time!
Saves money!**

The Jackson-mounted MINER EDGER (Trailer Type), originally built for exclusive use with the Jackson Lumber Harvester, is now available for sawmill operations.

This piece of equipment has many advantages which can increase your lumber profits. The Jackson-mounted MINER EDGER can be towed at 45 miles an hour behind an ordinary passenger car. You simply swing it into a handy position anywhere — in the yard, woodlot or forest.

You can set it up within 60 seconds, and it is immediately leveled and always in alignment. It runs independently of the head saw.

MINER EDGER SPECIFICATIONS

This edger is the famous MINER EDGER which can turn out 157 lineal feet of guaranteed straight lumber every minute.

In addition to steel spurs which guide every board straight, the MINER EDGER also features variable feed control with feed belt tightener.

Built to give years of trouble-free service, the MINER EDGER will pay for itself in an unbelievably short time.

Model 02-26", with 2-14" inserted saws and SKF Ball Bearing mandrel, is the standard model. All MINER EDGER models may be custom-mounted by Jackson Lumber Harvester, Inc. ... with or without engine.

Here are the special features of the Jackson-mounted MINER EDGER (Trailer Type): sturdy trailer frame, leveling jack, tow bar, spring-mounted axle for 6.00x16 tires, 25 hp. 4-cylinder Wisconsin Engine with clutch and adjustable base and a multiple V-belt drive.

Write for Prices and Delivery Dates

JACKSON LUMBER HARVESTER, INC.
BREWTON, ALABAMA

PRICE CHANGES EFFECTIVE FEB. 10, 1948
CONSUMER NET PRICES OF MINER EDGERS f. o. b. MERIDIAN, MISS.

If different, prices in effect at time of delivery will apply

Size 02-26", with 2-14" Simonds solid saws, babbitt bearings $294.00
02-26", with 2-14" inserted saws, babbitt bearings $325.00
02-26", with 2-14" inserted saws, SKF ball bearing mandrel (most popular for smallest mills) $376.00

The above Edgers will take rough-edge lumber 26" wide, and the two saws will open from 1½" to 12¼". Average shipping weight is 1200 pounds.

(Hoe or Simonds Saws Usually Furnished)

Size 2-30", with 2-14" Simonds solid saws, babbitt bearings $329.00
2-30", with 2-14" inserted saws, babbitt bearings $370.00
2-30", with 2-14" inserted saws, SKF ball bearing mandrel (most popular for small and medium mills) $410.00

The above Edgers will take rough-edge lumber 30" wide, and the two saws will open from 4" to 17". Average shipping weight is 1275 pounds.

Size 2-30", with 3-14" Simonds solid saws (two saws movable), babbitt bearings $377.00
2-30", with 3-14" inserted saws (two saws movable), babbitt bearings $437.00
2-30", with 3-14" inserted saws (two saws movable), SKF ball bearing mandrel (a popular edger) $475.00

The above Edgers will take rough edge lumber 30" wide, and the widest opening between the stationary saw and middle saw is 12¾". Average shipping weight is 1325 pounds.

(Hoe or Simonds Saws Usually Furnished)

Size 3-36", with 2-14" Simonds solid saws, babbitt bearings $316.00
3-36", with 2-14" inserted saws, babbitt bearings $427.00
3-36", with 2-14" inserted saws, SKF ball bearing mandrel $469.00

The above Edgers will take rough-edge lumber 36" wide, and the two saws will open from 1½" to 22¼". Average shipping weight is 1450 pounds.

Size 3-36", with 3-14" Simonds solid saws (two saws movable), babbitt bearings $434.00
3-36", with 3-14" inserted saws (two saws movable), babbitt bearings $495.00
3-36", with 3-14" inserted saws (two saws movable), SKF ball bearing mandrel $535.00

The above Edgers will take rough edge lumber 36" wide, and the widest opening between the stationary saw and middle saw is 18¾". Average shipping weight is 1500 pounds.

(Hoe or Simonds Saws Usually Furnished)

Legs and Leg Bolts: Sawmillers having portable mills usually furnish their own supports instead of buying Legs; add to price of Edger .... $ 55.00
Rope Lift Attachment for raising pressure rolls for edging lumber 3" thick and 4" thick extra .... $ 9.00
Hinged Side Rail for one width only (usually 4½") extra .... $ 6.00
Adjustable Side Rail from 3" to 6" .... $ 25.00

SEE OTHER SIDE FOR DESCRIPTION OF
JACKSON MOUNTED MINER EDGER (TRAILER TYPE),
FEATURING 25 HP 4-CYLINDER WISCONSIN
ENGINE (MOUNTED)

PRICE CHANGES EFFECTIVE FEB. 10, 1948

Sales Letter received 1949 from Jackson Lumber Harvester. Page 4

Attention . . .
Mr. Saw Mill Owner!

If you are a good saw mill man then you are a good filer, but *you can't beat*

THE DAVIS SAW FILER

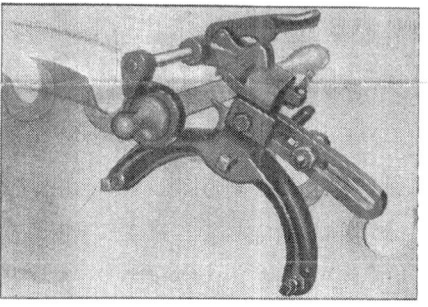

LEFT SIDE VIEW

This Filer was designed by a saw maker of many years experience, both in the factory and in the saw mill, who recognizes the fact that good saw filing is the most important factor in good saw milling.

There is many a saw that goes to the factory to be hammered when as a matter of fact if the teeth had been kept properly filed, it would have needed no hammering.

The Davis Filer is not intended to be used by the inexperienced mill man alone, but for the successful mill man as well, or the man who recognizes the fact that the daily output of his mill depends more on how his saw performs than anything else. It makes no difference how well you may be able to file your saw, you cannot do it with the accuracy that you can with this Filer.

This Filer will file every tooth absolutely accurate, save time in filing, alleviate swaging and make your teeth cut twenty to thirty per cent more lumber.

SOLD ON A MONEY-BACK GUARANTEE

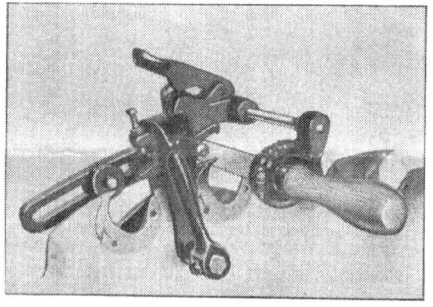

RIGHT SIDE VEIW

MANUFACTURED ONLY BY THE
CHATTANOOGA SAW WORKS
1512 Williams Street   CHATTANOOGA, TENNESSEE

Sales Letter received 1949 from Jackson Lumber Harvester. Page 5

Chapter Nine: Losing My Finger +

I guess I got a little ahead of myself. I have to go back to the summer of 1950. Susan was two years old, and Ardelle sewed dresses and clothes for her. Ardelle would sometimes come out to the sawmill wherever we were and bring Susan along and she just loved to play in the sawdust. Anyway this summer I had a dumb accident at the mill and got the end of one finger squeezed off by a v-belt. Because I was running a sawmill everyone thought I sawed it off but that wasn't the case. I will never forget that day; Johnny Graves was working for me so he took me to the doctor. The doctor didn't do much, just cleaned it up and bandaged it and said it will heal up in time but it is going to hurt. It hadn't hurt much up until then, but a while after I got home, he sure was right.

One amusing thing I remember from that day was I had brand new pair of yellow gloves on that morning when I got my finger squeezed. I knew I had squeezed my finger bad but didn't really know how bad because it didn't hurt the glove, but when I pulled the glove off, the end of my finger stayed right in the glove. After we got away from the doctor and were going home that new glove lay on the seat and you could feel the end of that finger in the glove. I guess I was sort of mad about the whole thing so I threw that new glove out the window. A dumb thing to do, but I did it. Since I have always thought if someone picked up that new glove and put it on and then felt the end of a finger in it, what a surprise it would be.

That finger really did hurt for a couple of days but it kept getting better, but it would have been hard to work on the sawmill, and the doctor said I shouldn't. We had been hoping to take a vacation going west and so we thought maybe this was the right time. So we packed up and took off. I had sold my 1939 Chevrolet 5-passenger coupe, a beautiful car, but I got a good price for it. I had bought a 1940 Buick straight eight, also a nice car. Somewhat of a gas hog but so what, gas was about .24 a gallon then.

So we made big plans and took off and left Francis my partner running the mill. It was an exciting time for us. I had never been west, nor traveled far except in the Army. Ardelle had traveled by train to Los Angeles the winter before we were married but other than that we had probably never been out of the states of Minnesota or Wisconsin. We really couldn't afford it, but the credit card years had already begun and we had one. We took a neighbor girl about 12 years old with us to help take care of Susan so Ardelle and I could have some time by ourselves. So we went off to the Black Hills, then to Yellowstone and then on to Seattle where Ardelle had an aunt that we could stay with for a couple days.

Another thing about that trip was I was still in the Army Reserves. As we were traveling we heard on the radio that the Korean War had started and reserves were being called for active duty. So it was kind of suspenseful, with the thought that I might have to go back in the Army. I think that made this vacation even more special to us.

The Buick was doing pretty well except going up the mountain grades it would get hot so we'd have to stop and let it cool off. When we got home I found out it had one weak cylinder so it really was running only on 7 cylinders, but we made the whole trip with no car troubles.

We had a couple good days in Seattle, then headed down to Puyallup, Washington and visited some people who had moved out there from Trade Lake. We then went down through Oregon State and on down the Redwood highway in California (that is a beautiful drive), then to San Frisco, a great place, then to Turlock, California where my cousin Mavis lived. She was the girl that helped Ardelle a lot with the wedding planning and work. Mavis had married a farmer from Turlock. She met him in Trade Lake when he came to visit his brother, who was Pastor at the Wood Lake Covenant church.

From there we went down to Los Angeles to visit the Johnson's, the ones Ardelle stayed with the winter before we got married, wonderful people. We had a great time. We have been lifetime friends. They were farmers from Roseau, Minnesota that moved out to California some years before.

Then we headed back east towards home. One memory of that night: we left in the evening so it would be cooler crossing the desert because it was really hot. I had a hard time to keep that 1940 Buick cool. We stopped for gas somewhere on the desert sometime in the night. It was still around 100 degrees, but the guy we bought gas from said, it's really cooled off it was 115 today. We never forgot that night.

Our next stop was in Denver, Colorado where we visited a fellow and his wife who I went to school with at Spirit Lake School. Just a one night stop, then on to Morris, Oklahoma and visited my

Army buddy and his wife. We were in Germany together. We were good friends in the army and have been right through to this day. We get together at least once a year. He and his wife are a great couple. He really was something else. I could write a book about him. His dad and his brother were in the oil business, drilling oil wells with part ownership in the wells they drilled. Jack didn't work with them when he first got out of the Army, but went to work for Sinclair in the northern panhandle of Texas. This was in the late 1940's or early 1950's.

Army buddy, Jack and his wife Velta Rae.

In those days of the oil fields and other businesses, the employer furnished housing for his employees. They built apartments, two apartments but only one bathroom between the two, so when you went to the bathroom, if your door wasn't locked you first made sure the door to the other apartment was locked.

Jack and Velta Rae lived in one of these apartments, and George Bush Sr. and Barbara lived in the one they shared the bathroom with. They were friends so they babysat for each other. So when George Bush Jr. got to be president, Velta Rae said, I changed diapers on that guy. Jack didn't work there too long but went back to Oklahoma and worked in partnership with his dad and his brother. I have been down there more than once when they were drilling with old fashioned drilling machines where you pound and then bale. It is pretty exciting especially when you are expecting to hit oil any minute. We have had many good times with them. We were there a couple a days then headed for home, back to the sawmill work, church, and enjoying being home.

After we had two girls, it was great to have a boy. He was quite a kid and still is as you will hear about later on.

If I have any regrets of those days, one would be that I didn't have enough time with my family. Two excuses: One, that the demand for our portable sawing lumber right on their place and because we could take on small jobs only a day or less on a place or months on a job, kept us with a list of dozens of jobs waiting for us. So we were working long days, usually about all the daylight hours, including Saturday. We didn't run the mill on Sundays. The other reason for working so much was we always were hard up so we needed to work and make as much money as possible, but Ardelle with Sibyl's help did a good job with the kids. So things were going pretty good in 1954-55-56. Then in September 1957 another son was born Dwight. So now we had 2 girls and 2 boys. Wow, what a family.

Susan, Kathy, Arlen, Dwight, 1957.

Ardelle was musical; she had a beautiful voice and sang in church a lot usually in duets, trios or quartet and in the choir. I was so proud of her, because she was musical she got Susan and Kathy started singing and they both took accordian lessons so they played and sang in church, as well as other places when they were really young. Kathy at this time was about 7 and Susan 9 or 10. I was a really proud Daddy.

My brother Bobby with Susan and Kathy. 1952.

Susan, Kathy, Arlen, Dwight, 1958.

Chapter Ten: Buying Birchwood Beach

Going back to 1955, there was a big change in our life. On Spirit Lake right across from Spirit Lake where I and all my family went to school and where my Dad and Mom went to school was a little resort; two cabins and a tumbling down dance hall that came up for sale. It had started in 1928 and kept growing (I could write a book about that place back then). The owner did have a beer license but they would bring in hard liquor and it got to be a wild place, with fights almost every Saturday night. Finally the town voted dry so he couldn't even have beer. This was I believe in the 1940's. From then on it went downhill, so it was really in bad shape by 1955. The owner had moved out west and they were trying to sell it, so the price kept coming down.

In about July of 1955 on a Saturday night in the barbershop, I heard they would sell for $6,000.00. The next day, Sunday, my sister Pearl and her husband, and Wesley, Ardelle's brother and his wife were at our place for dinner and we were talking about it. So we decided to go over and look at it. Spirit Lake in my mind is the most beautiful lake around. The place was named Birchwood Beach from the start (it still is Birchwood Beach Resort). It was run down, but it seemed the price was a steal so my two brother-in-laws said I was crazy if I didn't buy it and Ardelle was all for it because she had spent summers on a lake in Minnesota so she got all excited about it. So we bought it, we borrowed $1,000.00 from the bank to pay down and made payments to the owner on the balance.

So now we had bought Birchwood Beach. Our place in Trade Lake sold quickly, so we moved out to the lake in October of 1955. Right after we bought we decided to stay in one of the cabins over night. That night we had a terrible thunder and rainstorm and the roof leaked, and we couldn't move the beds so it didn't leak on them. So we had all the kettles, etc. on the beds to catch the water. It helped but you couldn't move or the kettle would spill. What a night!!! What a memory of our first night at Birchwood Beach. I don't remember how Susan and Kathy took it, so they must have been good, but I remember the thunder and rain was something else. What a start to a new home and a new endeavor.

    Ardelle was really the heart of it, she loved the lake and she loved people and we wanted it to be a Christian testimony to all who came to cabins or camp, by just being nice to them but not trying to be forceful. I will never forget Ardelle's Dad, he was a good man but very strict and he suggested we put a sign up on the road (Christians only) but this wasn't our idea. We wanted to show the beauty of God's creation and love to everyone.

Resort house as it stood for forty years, after being added to and remodeled a few times.

    So the clean up and work on the place began, because we needed to move in as soon as possible. Work on the house was No. 1 priority. My Dad and Ardelle's Dad both helped us a lot on the house, mostly after we moved. Much of the work was done in the next year or two, because I had some logs we sawed into lumber and that had to get dry before you could use them. Two reasons I did it this way: No. 1, I couldn't afford to buy lumber, and No. 2, I wanted it to be out of my own lumber. It was paneled with my own lumber, planed in Frederic of several species: ash, oak, maple, birch, etc. The den was a special show place with the knowledge and help especially of my Dad, and I learned a lot in the process. When I think back, I think Ardelle was really patient because with keeping the sawmill going, it took a long time to get it done. Besides that, the grounds and lakeshore needed a lot of work, dead and falling down trees to clean up, etc. One priority with Ardelle was the lakeshore. She worked so hard picking rocks and getting the weeds out. She was determined to make it beautiful and she did. I helped all I could.

    In the fall of 1955 and spring of 1956 we improved, painted, and put roofs on the two cabins that were there. Then in summer

The current owner of Birchwood Beach Resort, my son Dwight with his children, Corey and Heather in 1992.

of 1956 we built one new cabin. So in 1957 we had one new cabin to rent besides the two that were there. We didn't do anything with the dance hall until I think 1958, except to salvage lumber from it to use in the cabins. Then in 1957, we built another cabin. In looking back on it, I can't imagine how we got it done and kept the sawmill and lumber business going too.

Besides that, we had another addition to our family; Dwight was born September 26, 1957. Now we had two girls and two boys. Sibyl came and stayed a few weeks before he was born and a few weeks after. This was a big help to Ardelle; things were great. Then 4th of July 1959 Ardelle and I invited her whole family for the weekend. It was a time enjoyed by all.

Then on Monday I had a load of lumber to take down to Spring Valley, Wisconsin. Some of the family said she (Ardelle) had been working so hard she should go with me for the ride. It seemed like a good idea to us, so she went with. We got down there okay and were on the way home. They had been working on the road in one area so the road was really rough, we hit a really deep chuckhole and the front spring broke so that side of the truck fell down on the tire and caused the truck to jackknife and roll over in the ditch. She got thrown out and the truck rolled over her. I didn't get hurt much. There was a house nearby and I think they called the ambulance.

Ardelle was taken to the Baldwin Hospital, they did what they could but then she was taken by ambulance to a St. Paul hospital. I rode with in the ambulance and was with her to the end. I couldn't believe what had happened. One day everything was great, the next day she was gone and I was left with four kids: Susan, 11, Kathy, 8, Arlen, 5, and Dwight not quite 2. I did have good support from both her family and mine and friends. My brother-in-law Ray Hughes was a mortician in Hector, Minnesota. He and my sister Pearl just kind of took over for a lot of the funeral arrangements. It was really a big funeral. She was such a loving, caring beautiful young mother everyone that knew her loved her, I suppose partly because of her singing and sewing. She sewed a lot of the kids and her own clothes, besides more

In Loving Memory

Comfort

Oh, deem not
they are blest alone
Whose lives
a peaceful tenor keep;
The Power who pities man,
has shown
A blessing for the eyes
that weep.

The light of smiles
shall fill again
The lids
that overflow with tears:
And weary hours
of woe and pain
Are promises
of happier years.

ARDELLE ELAINE PETERSON

Born:
October 28, 1926
Died:
July 1, 1959
Age:
32 Years, 8 Months, 3 Days
Services:
Trade Lake Baptist Church
July 6, 1959 — 2:00 p.m.
Interment:
Union Cemetery
Trade Lake, Wis.
Clergy:
Pastor Lester Weko
Organist:
Iris Erickson
Songs:
Muriel Peterson, Alice Maki
and Almer Poulson
Pallbearers:
Donald Kramer
Wade Brask
Harlan Brask
John Graves, Jr.
Martin Larson
Lester Bergstrom

wedding dresses. Looking back at it I wonder how she found the time. Maybe it was because I was usually gone sawing about 12 hours a day five and a half days a week.

Our pastor was about our age, so it was really a hard funeral for him but he did a great job, sometimes with a choking voice and shedding tears. I found a song I wanted to be sung, "Today is Mine, Tomorrow May Not Come". Two of my younger sisters sang it; it was special.

Back to when she was dying. She was in a special care unit. Right when she died, our pastor and my brother-in-law Professor Russell Johnson and I were praying and I remember a really peaceful feeling came over me and I felt everything was going to be all right. Where we were praying was just a few feet from her bed, we stopped praying and I went to her and she had died while we were praying. This really upset me. So I rebelled against God and Pastor and Russell had a hard time with me. She had pulled the breathing tube out of her throat, so this maybe is why she died. It seemed maybe the special nurses weren't watching her close enough. In talking to the doctors afterwards, they convinced me her condition was so bad she couldn't have made it anyway.

One thing different about that time and now was I, with the help of my brother and I don't remember who else, dug the grave ourselves. And when they had put her in and put the cover on the vault and almost everybody had left, we filled the hole back. I remember like it was not long ago the feeling of shoveling the first few shovels over the vault. I'm not sure we needed to do this ourselves but it was maybe what I wanted and also it saved a few dollars.

So now the funeral was over. Ardelle was gone, but life for the living must go on. Ardelle's sister Margaret stayed with us a few days and my younger sisters helped some, but everybody was telling Sibyl "you have to go help them". I thought it was a good idea too. Pretty soon she did come and live with us and took over helping care for the kids, cooking, washing clothes, keeping house and helping with the resort work and correspondence. I don't know how I would ever have made it without her. She was great, the only part that was a little hard was that we both had great respect for each other but neither she nor I had any real love or feeling that we should get married, but some relatives and friends thought we should so sometimes it made it a little hard and even embarrassing. The kids loved her; she was like a second mom to them, but to my knowledge they never suggested we should get married. To them she was just Sib.

Sibyl with my sister Arlene's son Wayne in about 1990.

So times gradually got better; I missed Ardelle a lot, especially at night when I couldn't sleep. My days were so busy it kept my mind off of her. Then in 1960 something happened, that by 1961 changed my life forever.

Resort House 1990's.

Aerial photo of the sawmill.

Peterson Lumber semi.

Irene with Elmer, Mike, and Patty.

Chapter Eleven: Marrying Irene

Remember a few years back when I talked about when I first met Ardelle when Mabel Fisk brought her up to meet this GI she had known from before WW2 and she wrote to me when I was in the Army. Well, would you believe Irene, my loving wife now, was her younger sister; at that time she was only 15 or 16 years old. Their Dad worked for me a lot in those days. In my wildest dreams I never would have thought that the pretty live wire sister of Mabel's would ever be my wife.

Here is how it came about. Remember when I met Ardelle was in 1947 now this is 1960, thirteen years later. I don't know much of Irene's life in those years, but she was working in the Cities and a friend of hers took her with to Fairhaven, Minnesota for the weekend in about 1955 or 1956. Anyway, she met this young, good-looking farmer. I don't know if it was love at first sight or what, but in June, 1957 they got married. In December of 1958 Michael was born to Irene and Elmer.

Irene's picture in high school annual. Caption under it: "As brimful of mischief and wit and glee as ever a soul could possibly be."

Irene was busy being a farmer's wife, besides keeping house helping outside wherever needed. The chicken laying hens were one job left up to her. She had grown up on the farm but was a city girl for a few years, so this was getting back to nature. Elmer and his brother, along with their semi-retired dad were pretty big farmers. So it was hard work and long days, but they were newlyweds, so life was going great until the summer of 1960 when Elmer got sick in June. First they thought it was kidney infection, but the medicine didn't help, so they went down to University of Minnesota where he was diagnosed with cancer; they opened him up and found it was beyond help for what they could do at that time. Maybe the knowledge they have now would have made a difference. Anyway, they just sent him home to die. How sad, and Irene was pregnant. Patty was born August

7th and Elmer died Labor Day weekend. I felt so sorry for her.

The kids and I were close to their family, first because Irene's Dad worked for me, second because Irene's sister Lucille was married to my cousin and close neighbor Harland Brask. I did visit with Irene and Elmer a couple of times before he died. I did go to the funeral, but then I didn't see much of Irene until in March of 1961, when she came home to visit her folks and was in church on Sunday. She looked great and by that time I was kind of looking. I was kind of tired of being single with four kids. And I didn't want to marry Sibyl and she didn't want to marry me. So that was settled.

Anyway, Irene was staying over so I mustered up courage to ask her if I could take her out to eat on Sunday evening, and she said yes. That was the start of the last 42 years. I saw her off and on through the spring and summer, but a former pastor that we were good friends with was trying to help me find the right girl. They had a young widow in their

Irene and Carol, 1961.

church in Willmar, Minnesota who they thought was just the one for me. She was a nice lady but about three years older than me so that made her ten years older than Irene. Her name was Gloria; she had grandparents in Siren, Wisconsin about thirteen miles from Birchwood Beach. So when she came to see them it made it easy for us to see each other, but in the same spring Irene moved back here from Fairhaven and rented a place just a few miles from here so I could see her anytime and probably did almost every night.

But when Gloria came to Siren on weekends I wasn't sure what to do. She was a nice lady and I think I was learning to want Irene, but for a while I wasn't very sure, so I guess I was trying to sort it out by dating both of them. So a couple or more times I took Gloria out to eat on a Saturday night and then brought her to her grandparents and then quickly stopped in to see Irene before I went home to bed. This didn't go over too big with Irene, and I don't blame her. So the last time I did this when I stopped in to see Irene, I think she was kind of mad and she told me I better make up my mind now or she was through with me. So that was the last time I saw Gloria and I soon asked Irene if she would marry me. She said yes and then we started to make plans to make

Irene and Sibyl.

one family out of the two families.

It was Irene and Mike and Patty, me, Susan, Kathy, Arlen and Dwight, a total of eight and Sibyl, so that made nine. Sibyl had been with and done so much for us she was simply part of the family and Irene and I agreed she could live with us as long as she wanted to. She and Irene got along well and she was a big help and the kids all loved her. So once more they had a Mom and a Dad and Sibyl. What a family.

The problem was the house was now too small, so we quickly made plans and added on to the house. It was still a struggle financially because of the sawmill lumber and resort business. Irene realized some money from her marriage to Elmer, so that made it possible; also because I had some of my own lumber and material. We did have a local architect draw a plan that we liked, so we went with it. If that was now instead of then, the one thing that would be better is the insulation available is so much better now. But of course it was also a cost factor and my perhaps stupid idea that wood is cheap, so we would keep warm if we just keep the fire going well.

We made plans for the wedding for November 18th, 1961. This date was chosen so we could take

House after remodeling, 1961.

a honeymoon in deer season because deer hunting season in northern Wisconsin is a big affair, so it is hard to keep your men working when they want to be hunting, so the sawmill usually got shut down anyway. So it was a good time to get married. We do love to hunt deer too, but this was a special year; we both had our dear so we missed this hunting season for our honeymoon. At least it made a deadline to get the house done. We didn't get it all done but enough so we had our wedding in it with mostly family. We were all packed up so we left on our honeymoon the same night after the wedding and Sibyl was there to watch the family and keep the fires going and whatever needed to be

Our wedding, 1961. L-R: Carol's sister Pearl, Irene, Carol, Irene's brother Leroy.

done. We only went to Pine City that first night because we were really tired. I had kept working to get a little more done on the house until about five or six o'clock that same night.

The next morning we didn't get started too early, we had dinner in Mora, then headed west. Our first goal was Palouse, Washington where Irene's mother and her sister lived. We can't remember where we stopped that night but hoped to get to Palouse the next day, but it snowed and stormed all day, terrible driving. Somewhere in the mountains in western Montana all traffic was stopped; we got the only motel room left in town. It wasn't too much of a place but we were just glad to get a place to stop and get some sleep. We had been driving with chains on in deep snow for miles and it was still snowing hard. The next day when we woke up there was about two feet of snow on the cars. It was noon or so before we could get out and before they opened the highway west. So what, we were in love and on our honeymoon, so it didn't dampen our spirits too much so we headed west, but it was too late to get to Irene's mom that day. So we stayed somewhere and made it the next day.

We had a couple of good days there, then headed southwest through Washington and Oregon; this was interesting for me because we went through some of the towns my Dad used to talk about the days when he worked on the railroad and through Walla Walla, Starbuck and some others. This was sometime between 1900 and 1910, and at that time it was steam locomotives, fired with wood or coal and every stop had a water tank or tower so they could take on water for making the steam. The railroads changed from steam locomotives to diesel mostly in the

Family with 1959 Ford station wagon we drove on honeymoon.

1930s to 1950s. Dad started as a fireman and then engineer. The fireman's job was to put wood or coal into the firebox to heat the water to make the steam to make the engine to run. It was neat to go through the country he used to talk about.

We went on down through Oregon to northern California, Yreka, Weed, Mt. Shasta, Redding and on down to San Francisco. We spent one or two nights there, it was a very interesting city. Then we went back east to Turlock, California where my cousin Mavis lived; they were pretty big farmers and had acres of almond trees. Mavis and Joe had four boys, so it was a fun visit there. Then we continued on down the highway to Los Angeles, visiting the Johnson's, our friends from before Ardelle died. They are great people to show you a good time. Then on down to San Diego and a little into Tijuana, Mexico, then we headed back east to Phoenix, Tucson etc. We stayed in Albuquerque, New Mexico one night and did a little shopping in their downtown area, then on to Texas and Oklahoma and on to my army buddy and his wife. This was the first time they met Irene. We had a real nice visit with them and then headed back home and our family.

Building the sawmill in the early 1960's.

They had gotten along fine while we were gone. Christmas was coming up, and this was our first Christmas all together as one family. I don't remember too many details but it went fine.

One thing about that honeymoon trip: it didn't smell right away but after a few days when we had the heater on there would be a bad smell; we couldn't figure it out. We cleaned the car out and looked for what could be causing the smell a couple of times, but it was still there. After heading back east from Los Angeles across the desert it was over 100 degrees and the smell was terrible. I remember we stopped under a shade tree and took everything out of the car but couldn't find the smell. We used deodorizers to help a little. When we got home and told about it, the kids grinned and went down to the car and got a fish out they had stuck in the springs under the front seat. To this day I still don't know what that said about us getting married.

In 1962 I bought some more land to add to the resort and across the road to make room for the sawmill there so that we could set it up permanently and quit moving around.

View of the sawmill in the background, the horse corral at the resort in the foreground.

That same year we bought the Lundeen acreage, 130 acres. It had been their first home when the folks came from Sweden in the 1800's. It was beautiful, hilly, wooded land with some meadow and fields, beautiful for horseback riding trails and also a lot of timber that was ready to harvest. Lumber markets were good for those days and we did need money to keep things going.

We moved the sawmill right down in the woods and cut logs to saw into lumber; mostly hardwood that you could sell green to factories and they would kiln dry it and use it to manufacture whatever they were making: furniture, toys, whatever. After this we did move the sawmill home and started to buy logs and saw for the best markets: railroad ties, factory lumber, poorer grades for pallet material handling etc., but this gradually led us into manufacturing ourselves; pallets, skids, etc. to hopefully realize a better profit. This also created a need for more workers. In the late 1950's and into the 1960's we were hiring 3-4 men; by the 1970's and 1980's-1990's we had from 20 to 35 people on the payroll.

Jobs were not too plentiful in those days, so it wasn't hard to get help. Wages were really different in those days. In the early 1930's you could hire a man for a dollar a day or about .25 an hour, then in the war years, wages gradually went up. When I got out of the Army in 1946 and started sawing lumber with my Dad's mill, I was paying .60 an hour, then it kept going up. In 1950 they made the minimum wage .90 an hour. I had to be a registered employer and take out social security and withholding tax. I had this older man working who never would take more than .50 an hour. I explained to him that by law I had to pay him .90. He said okay, I'll give .40 to church. By the 1960's about which I'm writing now, I think I was paying about $1.25 an hour.

I'm sure if you never explained it this would seem ridiculous, but there is another side to the story. In the 1930's you could by a new car, Ford or Chevrolet, for under $400.00. By the late 1940's you could still buy one for about $800.00. Gas in the 1930's was, I remember, as low as .19 a gallon. After the war (late 1940's) it was around .29 a gallon. You could buy the best T-bone steak in a restaurant for about $1.65. Clothes and food and everything were really cheap compared to now. In this area you could buy a whole 40 acres of land for around $200.00.

By the fall of 1962 Susan, Kathy, and Arlen were in school in Trade Lake. This was the era when the small country schools were being closed. The idea was they could educate better and cheaper in bigger schools. I didn't agree with it then and I still don't, but that was the trend. Spirit Lake, Round Lake, and Big Trade Lake schools were already closed. Trade Lake was made part of the Frederic School District so it stayed open for a few more years. I think it closed in 1966, and they were all bused to Frederic. Arlen went six years to Trade Lake then to Frederic. Susan and Kathy went through eighth grade in Trade Lake and then to high school in Frederic. Dwight, Mike and Patty went all their school years to Frederic. A close neighbor drove the school bus for some of those years.

After we were married, I adopted Mike and Patty and Irene adopted Susan, Kathy, Arlen and Dwight, so we really were one family. Sometime in the fall of 1962, Irene realized she was pregnant and on April 30th, 1963, Wendy was born. This made us a family of seven. When Wendy was only a few weeks old, she got very sick. Irene took her to the doctor and he gave her some medicine and sent her home. He didn't seem to think it was very serious but she just wouldn't eat, so she got dehydrated. Irene called the doctor again but he still didn't encourage us to bring her in, but she got worse so we just took her in then. He bawled us out for not bringing her in sooner. This made me upset, so I had words with him. She was so sick for a while she was hanging in the balance. We stayed in the hospital all night with the doctor until the fever broke and she was out of danger. That night was a night neither we nor the doctor will ever forget. After that, Wendy got well pretty quickly.

Family 1962. Fun with the old buggy.

Irene and Carol.

Sawmill crew, 1980's.

Sawmill crew 1980. Carol and Irene made Christmas dinner for crew.

Inside the sawmill.

Chapter Twelve: Family Life and Daddy's Death

So Irene and our number one made a total of seven kids in the family and Sibyl was living with us too. So seven kids, Irene and I, and Sibyl made ten people in the house. What a zoo. But it was going pretty well, even though those years 1962-1963 were kind of emotional times for me because my Dad died. Even though I was almost 40 years old he was still Daddy to me. He was still farming, selling gravel and a busy man, struggling to make ends met with a big growing family. He had an accident, he was loading manure with a front-end loader on a John Deere tractor and it tipped over and one wheel came down on his head cracking his skull. He was in the hospital for a few days before he died.

I guess my Dad was my Hero. In my young years I thought there was nothing he couldn't do, build or fix. He made power units out of old cars or truck engines, building boats and snowplows. He made sleds for his own kids as well as other relations. To this day I don't know how he did it. And when I got back out of the Army and got into sawing lumber, threshing etc. he always was my advisor, problem solver and helper. I don't know how I would have made it without his help.

Dad in 1925.

I have very vivid memories of how he helped people in all kinds of ways. He was town chairman in Trade Lake quite a few years in the 1930's. In those years the town board was sort of the relief board also. So if any one family needed food, clothes, firewood or whatever, that was up to the town board to decide how to help them. Daddy didn't believe much in using town funds, especially since there wasn't much. So he would try to help in some other way, like getting them to work for the town or whatever so they could make it on their own. But to help them out a little he would bring them some potatoes; something we always had. Every year we would have two or three acres of potatoes; he had built a really good cellar, so the potatoes kept well, so we had our own potatoes the year around to eat, sell or give away.

He wasn't an outspoken, religious man but he had ways of saying things that showed his faith and was a testimony. One memory I have of this, in the dry years every bit of hay you could come up with was needed. So this was maybe part of the reason we cut with the horse mower or with a scythe every bit of grass all along the road ditches along the fences where the cows couldn't reach it. Then we would rake as much as we could with the horse dump rack, rake the rest by hand with a homemade wooden rake, then haul it into the haymow. The result was our roadside all along the two sides of our 160 acres looked beautiful. I remember someone was asking him in Swedish why he did this. They were speaking Swedish, so I can't say it just like he did; he gave the reasons that we needed the hay, etc., but more importantly that we are put in this world to make it beautiful, and we should leave it more beautiful than it was before we were here. Anyway, I do have so many memories of my Dad. I did really miss him and still do.

I believe it was in 1963 that we built the store on the resort, the same two guys that helped build the cabins in 1957 did most of the construction, but Irene and I did a lot of the finishing etc. It was needed for supplies, etc. for the tourists, but we thought we could get enough business from around the lake and community to make it a complete grocery, souvenirs, and fishing tackle store, just for the summer tourist season. It did okay for a few years but with the big chain stores coming in it wasn't paying to have a complete grocery line so we gradually dropped off to just basic needs.

Irene in the resort store, 1960's. Note the big fish.

Around this time, we bought a Welch Shetland pony, the people who had him had named him Dynamite. It was a good name for him, because that was what he was. He was really fast, and he was gentle, but he could also be mean and hard to catch. I had bought a real nice top buggy that we hitched him to and had a fun time. But one time Susan and a cabin girl from Illinois had hitched him up and were playing frontier day and they got into some bees and had a runaway. They tipped the buggy over but didn't get hurt. The buggy was still okay but the nice top was wrecked. We still have the buggy, but no top. After that we used him more for riding, he was really fast but hard to stop.

I think Kathy was only about 10 years old the first time she raced in the pony races at the St. Croix and Grantsburg fair. Dynamite always got first place.

Kathy on Dynamite in Centennial costume, 1964.

He would get so hyped up when they were going to start that I would have to hold on to him behind the other ponies, then when they shot the starting gun I would let go and in just a little while they would be in the lead. Then I would take off running across the racetrack to help Kathy stop him after he went past the grand stand. There was only one pony that could get close to beating Dynamite. It was a boy riding him and he sure did want to beat Kathy, but he never did. It made it really exciting.

I guess Dynamite was really the start of horses at Birchwood Beach. He was three years old when we got him and lived to be thirty-four years old. He was a legend. We kept getting more horses so were pretty soon giving trail rides, and until Kathy got out of high school she led and managed the trail rides. About the same time we bought Dynamite, we bought a beautiful palomino mare that was Susan's horse. I guess it had been trained by an Indian. It was so well trained she could ride it bareback with no bridle or anything and still have complete control.

Postcard from early years of Birchwood Beach.

But the sad part was it somehow got lead poisoning and died before we had it very long. That was really a sad time for the whole family, but especially Susan.

Around this time, we built a small hip roof barn. We built it especially for horses that were going to foal, but also as a little show place of the traditional hip roof red barn and also some hay storage in the haymow. Irene and I built that ourselves. It was for horses for a few years then we converted it to recreation room both downstairs floor and second floor hayloft. Then somewhere in the seventies we made bathrooms, with men's on the lower floor and ladies upstairs with showers, flush toilets etc. Until that time we only had pit toilets in the upper campground. We had built a shower house in the lower campground. At the same time we put in water, electric and sewer to all the trailer spots in the lower campground.

The red hip roof barn Carol and Irene built.

The 1960's must have been the busiest years for all that happened. Getting married to Irene, putting the families together, all the building projects and it was also the years Irene went to beauty school from 1967 to 1970. She attended three winters, then graduated and became a licensed beautician. She would leave on Sunday night or early Monday morning and come home Friday night. Susan was working in the Cities and Irene stayed with her some of the time or with a friend. Then she worked part time at some beauty shops around home. I have never had a haircut in a barbershop since she went to beauty school. Pretty good, huh?

Then besides that, the 1960's were when all of our girls were born. Wendy in 1963, then in 1965 Wanda arrived. All three of our girls were and are very special, but Wanda with her smile, outgoing personality and love for everyone and everything was something else, especially from the time she could walk. One thing we especially remember was a couple had a trailer close to the house and she had made good friends with Wanda. When Wanda was about two years old, when she got up in the morning, she would soon have to go visit her. She would knock on her door, and when the lady opened it, Wanda would say "What doing?"

Family 1966. Back L-R: Mike, Dwight, Arlen. Front L-R: Patty, Kathy holding Wanda, Susan holding Wendy.

Another remembrance is we sometimes would have a Saturday night fun variety show. I would put my semi-trailer flat bed for a platform and make steps to get up on it of railroad ties from the sawmill waiting to be hauled. We would lift the piano up on the trailer with the forklift. Anyway, this one time two guys, one dressed like a girl, were doing a comedy song and Wanda slowly went up the steps on the platform dragging her blanket. When she got up there and was pointing at the guys singing, the crowd was roaring with laughter. The guys singing hadn't noticed Wanda so they thought the laughing was for them and I'm sure it was somewhat, but Wanda kind of stole the show.

I think it was that summer we went on a camping trip to Wisconsin Dells. We left Wanda home with a neighbor friend, but we were still nine bodies in a tent. But we had a good time.

The sawmill lumber and pallet business kept going and I was still the only head sawyer on this mill. My brother Bob had the other permanent mill at Ridgeland, Wisconsin. Anyway, the sawmill was where I spent most of my time. I don't know how we got everything done.

In 1966, Susan graduated from high school. For the last couple years of high school, she worked part time as a nurse's aide at Grantsburg Hospital; she loved it and decided she wanted to be a nurse. So in the fall 1966, she started nurse's training in Eau Claire, but after a few months for some reason she decided not to be a nurse and went to Minneapolis and to work as a telephone operator. So she had an apartment rented and had room for one to live with her. I think maybe this was partly the reason Irene decided to go to beauty school, since she could stay with Susan during the week, and it had also been a dream of hers. That went fine, but then the winter of 1967, Bruce came home from Vietnam and Susan and Bruce fell in love and were married in summer of 1968. Bruce grew up here, but he went in the army and went to Vietnam. That was a terrible war and was really hard on Bruce. Their getting married meant Irene had to find a different place to live while going to beauty school.

Then in September of 1969, Tammy was born, a beautiful baby girl. This made ten people again in our house. But not for long, because in 1968 Kathy graduated from high school, so she soon went to college in St. Paul.

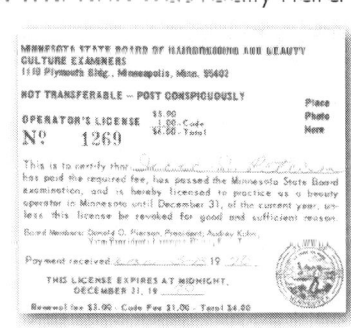

Irene's beauty certificate.

Sawmill crew at work. Dwight and Mike are on top of a pallet on a John Deere high lift fork lift for loading semi.

Susan and Kathy with horses and old buggy.

Susan with Inka and her colt Velvet.

L-R: Irene, Carol's sister Dorothy, Sibyl. 1980's.

Two of my sisters with their children in the 1950's. L-R: Dorothy holding Darla, Arlene behind Wayne and Rodney.

Brothers and sisters in front of the old pumphouse in the 1970's. L-R: Dorothy, Arlene, Bernice, Carol, Pearl.

108

Chapter Thirteen: Sawmill, Pallet Business +

In the late 1960's and into the 1970's, the demand for material handling, lumber, pallets, skids, etc. really kept us busy. We were still doing all our nailing by hand. This made a good job for the boys, even though they were only from 11 to 14 years old. I paid them piece-work, so the more pallets or skids they made, the more money they made. This was good for them and me too. They could earn and save to buy bicycles, mini-bikes, snowmobiles or whatever. It also was good for me because all the laws regarding labor etc. weren't made yet.

This is one big thing that I think has helped to ruin our country. There are too many laws saying you can't use young help; this has left young people with too much time on their hands to goof around and get in trouble. My boys and some of their friends really learned to work here, but now I believe our stupid lawmakers have done much to ruin the attitudes, morals, etc., of our young people. I have always maintained that if kids don't get some hands-on experience about work, safety, etc., by the time they are 18, I think it is too late. This of course will be different with different kids and parents.

100 years ago there was so much less technology like computers, TV etc. I'm not saying these advancements

Mike, Dwight, and Arlen painting oars for the resort boats.

are all bad, but I am afraid they are more bad than good. I sincerely believe that perhaps the most damaging thing to our children and our society is the ACLU (American Civil Liberties Union) and I believe it is Government funded.

I believe at the start of it, the idea was to make everything fair and free to everyone to do and think as they please. But I believe it has gotten way out of hand, to what is taught in school has been changed as much as they can to not teach history as it was and not to mention God or be able to pray. It is so sad. There is some hope because several lawsuits against the ACLU have been won in the last years; that is encouraging.

Our country was founded on Christian principles. I am sure

not all of the historic men who framed our constitution believed exactly alike but they did agree that a belief in God was needed to make a good country. I believe they did God's will; oh, it wasn't perfect and still isn't perfect. I admire Abraham Lincoln and his leadership through the Civil War, bad as it was; but I believe that too was in the will of God to make this a better country. Also how the native Americans have blended into our society has made our country better.

To get back to the last 100 years or so; the schools in this area were being started and built from the 1880's on, and that is when the Spirit Lake School was built where my Dad, Mother and Ancestors went to school and it is where my sisters and I went in the late 1920's and 1930's. What was taught in school then was mostly the three R's: reading, writing, and arithmetic, with some history, etc. There were no computers, and usually one teacher did the whole thing with the help of the older students, but I really believe we learned more of what we really needed to know than what the kids are learning now.

Life went on, and now we are in the 1970's. It is really harder for me to remember a lot of things that happened from the 1960's and on than the 1950's and back. In 1972, Arlen enlisted in the Army. There were threats of war in those days so he ended up in Germany before the end of 1972. He did very well in training in California and then at Fort Knox, Kentucky, as well as in Germany. Would you believe he was in the same area I was in after WWII in the Army Occupation.

I had always hoped to get back to Germany sometime, so in March of 1973, Irene and I flew over there to see Arlen. It was quite the trip for us; we had flown very little and could hardly afford it. We flew from Minneapolis to New York, then on to Frankfurt, Germany. When we got to Frankfurt, the airfield had so many planes ahead of ours to land, our plane couldn't wait because it had to go on to Turkey or somewhere, so they landed in Copenhagen, Denmark instead. They treated everybody that was supposed to land in Frankfurt royally. They had a bountiful meal, the likes of which we had never experienced before. Then they took us on a bus tour around

Irene with Arlen in Frankfurt.

Copenhagen. It was quite the sight seeing tour. Then, after about five hours, they got us on a plane back to Frankfurt. Quite a free addition to our trip!

But, of course, Arlen was waiting for us in Frankfurt in the morning and we didn't get there until about eight that night and he couldn't seem to find out what happened to us. He called home a couple of times and talked to Sibyl, but all she knew was that we had left. I guess he finally found out, so he was waiting when we got there. He had rented a car so we got out of the airport pretty quickly and found a motel and stayed the first night. Then we headed south for the Army Base where Arlen was stationed. We stayed in a Holiday Inn overnight and Arlen went to his base overnight.

In the morning, we started out for Birches Garden, a ski resort that had been taken over by the U. S. Military in WWII. The U.S. military

Arlen and Carol at Birches Garden.

still had it as a vacation place for the G.I.'s, and Arlen had a reservation there. It was quite the place close to Switzerland and Austria. It is a beautiful place high in Bavaian Alps with beautiful high and long ski slopes. They had been having rainy, foggy weather and the slopes were icy, so it was sort of treacherous skiing. They didn't have any grooming or snowmaking equipment, so it was just dependent on new snow coming, and it didn't come. We still had a good time for three days, then we headed south through Austria and down into Italy.

That was a day and night I'll never forget. Austria is beautiful but as we got into Italy heading for the city of Florence it got really foggy, you could hardly see anything and we couldn't find anywhere to stop. We finally made it safe to Florence quite late and we needed a place to eat and sleep. We probably were in the wrong area but we did get a room and restaurant, but it was different. It seemed half of the people in there had dogs, and the food: yuck. In the morning, we drove around Florence sight seeing; we did see the water canals and boats right in the city. It wasn't as romantic and beautiful as the picture we had seen.

Then we headed across Italy to Pisa where the leaning tower is; that was really interesting. We stayed there one night, then headed up the Mediterranean coast and back into France.

Irene and Arlen in front of Leaning Tower of Pisa.

This was beautiful: driving high above the Mediterranean looking down on the French Rivers, then on to Marseilles, France. Marseilles is where a lot of soldiers went for furlough in WWII. I never got there then so I wanted to now. It was OK but not quite what I had dreamed.

We stayed there one night then headed up to Paris; about a day's drive. We got close enough so we could see the Foshay Tower, kept going until we got real close to it and there was a Hilton Hotel there. At first they said they didn't have any rooms but after a while we did get rooms. This was a pretty fancy place. The next day we went up in the Foshay Tower. It was quite a climb but a fun experience, pretty high and kind of scary. The next day we did a little driving around and a little shopping but I don't think we really got downtown Paris. Driving there was really wild.

The next day we headed back east toward Germany. I think it was about the same way I went with the Army 28 years before, only that was by train. We crossed the Rhine and stayed in or close to Heidelberg. This is where I spent quite a bit of my Army days and where Hildy lived. Arlen had looked her up before and had visited her a couple of times. He said she was just as beautiful as the pictures I had of her from when I was over there. She was still living there, but we didn't find her that day, but I got a chance to show Irene and Arlen around the town, go up in the castle etc. where I had been 28 years ago. This was the day before we had to be back at Frankfort and fly home.

That night we did get Hildy on the phone so we talked to her. Arlen talked to her, but she seemed to want to talk to me most. Ha. I did care a lot for her but I loved Ardelle and I love Irene.

Irene and Carol by rented car in Marseilles.

But, I can't help wondering what my life would have been like if that soldier that was supposed to transfer our mail had not fooled her. I still believe it probably was supposed to be this way, because I still wonder if she could have handled the change she would have had to face to come to northwest Wisconsin and live with a hard working Swede.

This was our last night in Germany. The next day Arlen brought us to Frankfort and we got on the plane for home and he went back to his Army days. We had the trip of a lifetime. We dream of going back to Germany again, but when you're 80 years old, it will probably be just a dream.

Arlen, Dwight and Mike worked hard making skids, etc., but they always had projects of their own going. Before Arlen went in the Army, he was always building or rebuilding some kind of jalopy or buying and fixing old cars. Dwight got good at cutting and welding, and building kites to fly behind a boat, building air boats, etc. The three boys were all good at driving the forklifts, putting logs on the mills, moving lumber slabs, and loading the semi long before they were 15 years old. Arlen drove semi quite a bit before he went in the Army. Dwight drove my semi continuance from when he graduated from high school until the 1990's.

Dwight, Carol, Scott Larson (Susan's son) in door of the semi, mid-1970's.

The big changes in this country before the 1950's are the ones I remember the most. They were in my mind some of the best years of my life, in spite of hard times of the 1920's-1930's and sad times but also good times. It seemed after World War II things started going bad as far as Christian Morals and what was right and wrong.

I talked to a former pastor in 1990 or so about the changes that have happened since the end of WWII as far as lifestyles, morals, abortion, divorce rates, sexual abuse, etc. He surprised me by saying "You veterans of WWII are somewhat to blame for it." The more I thought about that the more I thought he maybe was at least partly right.

When I first got overseas in France and then in Germany it seemed so bad compared to what I had known at home, because of community, church and parents. It didn't lead me astray, but I can't say I never was tempted. So many of the G.I.'s didn't have a growing up life similar to mine, and when they got home to young wives and friends and family, it perhaps was a factor in the way morals, sex, drinking, etc., got worse and worse. Then as it got into our government, the trend drifted away from the dependence on faith and belief in God that our country was founded on, and it got really bad.

When I grew up, sex was for after marriage. I'm not saying everybody was good, but when they weren't, it was downplayed instead of as it is now, when anything seems to be okay. If it feels good, it's okay. I believe that is why so many women and girls get pregnant and then want to have abortions. When I grew up, if a girl got pregnant out of marriage it was kept as quiet as possible. Now it seems anything is okay. It is really sad the way it is. I believe the ACLU (American Civil Liberties Union) is very much to blame for this, as well as a lot of other things, like taking God out of schools, taking our Christian Heritage out of our history books, trying to get In God We Trust off our money, forcing judges to take the Ten Commandments down, etc. The Supreme Court is so wrong in most ways, but the Democratic Party seems to go for all these wrongs. This is where my thoughts and efforts have been and are these days. Some of these things haven't happened yet, and hopefully they won't if we conservative Christians keep fighting.

Another big reason it is hard for me to write about the changes in the last 50 years is that so much of it has been in technology: computers, cordless phones, etc. Everything, even car motors, machinery of every kind is operated by new technology, and this is where I am ignorant. It has gotten to the point that it doesn't pay to service, change oil, etc., in your own car because you don't have the knowledge or proper equipment to do it. I think this is why old timers like me look back at our younger years and think of them as the best in almost all ways.

Irene and Carol on trip to Europe. Dress Irene has on is the one Carol bought her there. She still has that dress today.

Chapter Fourteen: Business and Finances

I want to try to picture what the financial situation for small businesses was in the 1970's, especially for us. The sawmill business was growing and the demand for our lumber and pallets etc. seemed endless, but we were always hard up; we didn't have the capital we needed. It seemed the banks were really afraid of small businesses because so many small businesses failed, and sawmills and the wood industry rated as one of the riskiest. Another thing was that the college advisers felt that becoming a lawyer was about the best business to be in to make a lot of money easily, and so too many young people decided to be lawyers looking for work. At the same time the lawmakers kept making more and more liability laws and so Workers Compensation Insurance kept going up and up, and it still is. And there are too many lawyers, so lawsuits are really out of hand.

To get back to our situation; we were always hard up and in need of more capital. In those years from the early 1970's to 1990 we were doing a gross business of 1 to 3 million dollars a year, but at the same time we kept needing to invest in more machinery, trucks, etc., with no reserve money and very little chance to get any. Perhaps part of the problem was me. I had faith in what we were doing and faith that things were getting better, but I was too conservative. If we needed say $20,000.00 to do what we were trying to do, I felt sure the bank wouldn't loan us that much, so I would think maybe we can make it with $15,000.00 and so I'd ask for that, then the bank would loan us only $10,000.00. Every little bit helped, so we went ahead as if we had gotten the $20,000.00. This added to the struggle with a big growing family.

It was never easy all the years since we bought Birchwood Beach in 1955 until maybe the 1980's we operated Peterson Lumber and Wood Products and Birchwood Beach Resort together on one checking account. This had advantages and disadvantages, Birchwood Beach was growing because more and more people wanted to have all season rental spots for their recreational trailers.

Carol in pallet factory, 1975.

This was great because the season lease rent usually was more than you could make renting overnight, weekends, etc., and we had a lot of beautiful hilly hardwood area (mostly hard maple) above the lake that was still undeveloped. So when someone would come and want a season spot and we didn't have any available we would go up in the hilly area and figure out where we could make another spot. So that is how what we call the upper campground came to be.

One story I like to tell about this is regarding when we first bought more land and were wondering how we should develop it. The state of Wisconsin had a so called specialist to advise how to make a campground. So I contacted him to come and look and give us some advice. He came and we walked up in the hills and beautiful maple trees, other hardwoods, and pine. We didn't go far before he said "I don't see how you can make a campground out of this unless you cut all these trees and get big bulldozers and bulldoze it flat and then make it into a campground." I told him we might as well not waste any more of your time because that will not happen.

Carol's semi with a load of railroad ties going to Superior.

Now people often compliment us on that this is the most beautiful campground, and how did you plan it? My answer is we didn't really plan it, it just grew a little every year because of people wanting to come and stay, and with help from us with developing the spots one at a time. The equipment we had for the mill also helped: forklifts, loaders, bulldozers etc. This made it easer to make roads, develop spots, and get electric and water wherever needed.

I'm sure there were quite a lot of man hours paid for by Peterson Lumber for work on the resort. Besides, lumber, timber, etc. used on the resort that came from Peterson Lumber was free. That was both good

A season lease trailer at Birchwood Beach.

and bad. Good because it helped Birchwood Beach grow; bad because it cut the profit margin on Peterson Lumber, which in itself was also both good and bad. Good because it made less income tax to pay, but bad because the bankers always look at your profit margin if you want to borrow money.

This was our situation, but small business had always had a hard time getting finances for several reasons. The programs that were supposed to help small businesses were not set up to really help a true small business with a potential of 10 employees or less. They call it small business assistance, but they wouldn't really consider your application if you had less than 50 employees.

A government funded organization called Impact 7 was started to help this area because It was designated to be a poor area (which it was). Impact 7 was seven counties and the Indian reservation. Each county had I think three board members and the Indians had three board members. I was on that board from Burnett County for I don't recall how long. So there were a total of 24 board members and the government paid managers. One of our responsibilities was to work on applications for loans for small businesses. When as a board we would agree that a loan should be made for some small business, then it would go to Washington to be approved or denied, and it usually was denied.

Once there was a meeting when this person (a young lady) who could approve or deny what the board had approved was there to speak and she was under 30 years old. This was when I decided it was time for me to get off the board. We were giving our time for free, but it seemed we didn't really have any say, 24 people that one young lady could decide against us. Another thing that angered me was, the manager said "well at least it makes a job for me and my paid help." Impact 7 is still around, and the biggest thing they have accomplished is helping the Indian Reservation get the casinos going. I don't like this either, since I don't believe in gambling because it teaches people that if they're lucky, they can get something for nothing.

Semi loaded with pallets.

To get back to the reality of those days, the 1960's and on. We never had much money in the bank and always had too much debt, but looking at those years they were some of the best years of our lives. They also must have been the busiest years with the sawmill, lumber and pallets business growing, needing more machinery, buildings, etc., and in need of more help. From the 1960's to the 1990's we had 20 to 35 people on the payroll. Until the mid-1970's, Irene and I did the managing and office work, payroll, etc., with some help from the girls, especially Wendy. The boys were part of the mill crew when not in school. Then Arlen enlisted in the Army in 1972 at just 17 years old.

In spite of the business keeping us busy those years we did manage to take a few family trips. Once to Oklahoma to visit my buddy, once to California, and to Florida three or four times. In Florida we enjoyed the Florida Keys the most, and we went to the same place two or three different years. This was after Susan and Kathy and the boys didn't go along, but I remember Sibyl was living with us so she took over when we were gone. We were really blessed to have her in our lives.

There are so many memories of those trips, one memory is when there was a gas shortage, so most of the gas stations weren't open at night. We usually started out at night and drove all night; I had the car full when we left, and since some Wisconsin stations were open after midnight I thought it would be the same in Illinois. But it wasn't. We kept going until in the middle of the night we ran out of gas right on the freeway in Chicago. It was winter and cold; thank goodness there was not much traffic. There were lights ahead that we thought might be an open gas station. So Wendy steered the car and Irene and Patty and I pushed it. A highway maintenance man came along and he had some gas in five gallon cans but he said he couldn't sell more than three gallons. The trouble was he didn't have any way to measure it or pour it in our car, so I think we spilled a good part of the three gallons, but we did get going.

One of our Florida trips, 1973. L-R: Irene, Wanda, Tammy, Patty, Wendy.

At that point, it still wasn't morning, and we still couldn't find a gas station open. We got through Chicago into Indiana heading south toward Indianapolis and ran out of gas again. It was getting towards morning so there was some traffic both ways but I couldn't get anybody to stop. Then I noticed an old semi like mine at home coming from the south and it seemed to be slowing up, so I ran across the median and he stopped and asked if I needed help. I said "I'm out of gas," and he said "Get in with me, I know where we can get some back up the road about 10 miles." On the way up there, he told me he had a radio in his truck and a guy with a semi going south had told him there was a station wagon up the road with a bunch of kids in the car that must need help, so he was watching for us. Wasn't that nice?

Anyway, we got up to the station he knew would be open. He talked to the man at the station who said he could sell us five gallons of gas and take me back to our car. The driver of the semi got back in his rig; I offered to pay him, but he wouldn't take anything. So all I could do is say "Thank You," then I had to wait a little until the station guy closed the station while he took me back to our car. I paid him for the gas and tried to give something for his trip and trouble, but he refused to take any money. I will never forget those two guys. Afterwards, we headed on south to Kentucky, Tennessee, Alabama, and Florida, but I will never forget the experience and the goodness of people.

I have so many memories of family trips, but also many memories of driving my own semi, on business trips for Peterson Lumber or Birchwood Beach or School Board trips. I sometimes picked up hitchhikers; considered a no-no now and even then. I did it because back in the 1930's there were people hitchhiking because they needed to get somewhere but didn't have a car or money, but were honest people, victims of hard times of those years.

When I picked up a hitchhiker, as soon as he got in I questioned him where he was going and why, etc. Sometimes this led to some very interesting stories. If they didn't want to tell me anything, I tried to let them off as soon as possible, but I don't remember any bad experiences, except maybe one that was perhaps both good and bad.

One cold winter day I was heading up to Superior, Wisconsin with a load of railroad ties from the sawmill that we sold to a treating plant (we sawed a lot of railroad ties in those years). When I was about 25 miles from Superior I noticed an old man

Peterson Lumber semi.

in a suit carrying a suitcase heading south looking really cold. I thought if he's still walking when I come back I'll pick him up when I'm heading home. Sure enough he was, so I stopped and asked him if he wanted a ride. He said yes, but he was so cold I had to help him get up in the cab of my old International.

As soon as we got going down the road I started to question him, but at first he was so cold he could hardly talk. Once he warmed up enough, he said he was from Wyoming. I said "Do you mean Wyoming, Minnesota?" He said "No, I am from Wyoming." So I asked him why he was hitchhiking here in this cold. He said "You should have been a lawyer the way you ask questions, but I will try to tell you the whole story." Some of the story was true and some wasn't but I didn't know that for more than a year. So I pretty much believed it all at the time.

He said he owned a ranch in Sundance, Wyoming. He had been in the hospital for some operation on his head; this maybe was true because he had a couple of bandages on his head. He had a very special nephew in Canada across from Detroit who had cancer and was dying and he wanted to see him before he died. His wife didn't want to go so he went alone on the train. He saw his nephew and was on the way home, when he rented a room in Windsor just across from Detroit. That night somehow his billfold and his money were stolen. He had only a little change and the police couldn't or wouldn't help him, so he walked across to Detroit and then walked and hitchhiked through Michigan to Superior.

The night before I picked him up, a priest took him in and gave him a bed and breakfast and 50 cents and sent him on his way. This was his story; as we got down to Siren he wanted to get out, he said he had a son in Hawaii that if I just would borrow him a little money he would call him and they would figure it out. It was so cold (below zero), and some of his story didn't seem to fit. So I said "No, come home with me and get some supper and we'll see what we can do."

I told him he could call his son from my house, but he didn't seem to want to do that. So we ended up renting a room for him in Frederic and loaning him enough money to take a bus to the Cities the next day and a train ticket back to Wyoming and Sundance. He was so grateful and said as soon as he got home he would send us the money. The money didn't come, so I had our sherrif check with the police in Sundance and they knew of him, but didn't know where he was now. I sent a letter to him but it came back refused. It wasn't only the money but the fact that it seemed I had been fooled.

That next winter we took a trip out west to visit Irene's sister and mother and then on to to California. So I decided we'd stop in Sundance and see what we could find. We left the kids in the motel and we went to Sundance. Sundance is just a small town, probably only one restaurant. We went to get some breakfast and ask some questions. There were quite a few people in there and some of them knew him but didn't know where he was now. The story of owning a ranch wasn't true but he had worked on one. I went to the Post Office and showed them my letter that had been returned refused. The postal person said he did know of him but didn't know for sure why he had marked it refused. Anyway, I never did get my money back, but I don't feel bad. It was quite an experience.

I had other similar experiences that I could write a book about, but I don't regret any of them. One of my cousins and a good friend always kidded me for being a soft touch.

A show picture of a
load of logs.

Building the tree house in 1962. It slept 6 or more people, and stood for about 15 years.

Carol with his tractor bringing in wood.

Resort church service.

Chapter Fifteen: Campground Church Services +

Another event started in the middle 1960's and still happens every year from Memorial Day Sunday through Labor Day at our Birchwood Beach Resort. We have had Interdenominational open air church services on the patio by the house from 10:00 am to 10:45 am with coffee, milk and a snack, plus a visiting and getting acquainted time. We always had special music from campers, friends, relatives, etc.

The speaker has very seldom been a ordained preacher but someone with a testimony and story of their life. As the years went by many of them have enjoyed coming back once a year even if they aren't camping here anymore and the campers, neighbors, etc. enjoy hearing them again. Often it seems you get a message that is more touching, more blessed than you get in your own church, where you mostly have the same speaker all the time. Our services seldom have the same speaker or music more than once in the season.

Carol and sister Arlene at the front.

Sometimes we have been asked why we have it at the same time most churches have their services. We have considered and prayed about this. I guess the main reason is that most people come camping for a good time and that is what we want them to have, but traditionally Sunday morning is for church and so whether they have a home church or not, this is when they are most likely to take time from whatever they are doing and come to our outdoor church services. Often our campers express to us how they have enjoyed the services and received a blessing. Sometimes someone will tell us that because of coming to our outdoor service they have gotten more involved in their own church, or even sometimes if they didn't have a home church they now have one.

One thing Irene and I used to do on Saturday nights was go around the campground and visit and invite campers to come to the service on Sunday morning. Especially on Saturday nights, there are dozens of campfires and people enjoying them. It was a good time for us and we got to know a lot of our campers,

Irene in front of some campers in winter.

but as the campground grew it seemed like Saturday night wasn't enough time to get around before many of them were in bed. Anyway, we haven't done that so much in the last few years. I'm not sure if it is just we are too busy or just getting old!!!

Having these outdoor church services pretty much at the same time as most churches has kept us away from our own church in the summer on Sunday mornings, but we do keep in touch and it's really nice to get back to our own church in the fall.

These outdoor church services were somewhat in the dream stage of my first wife Ardelle and I even before she was killed in 1959, but then nothing happened until around 1965 when a season lease camper helped us get it started. His wife played the piano, so we moved the piano out on the patio every Sunday morning and back in again. He led them for two or three years, then another camper that was very musical helped us. My memory is not very good but I did lead the services for a number of years but the older I got the harder it was for me to talk about some things and my lips would quiver so I couldn't say what I wanted to. So it would embarrass me and my family. Anyway the last ten years or so Lydell (Wendy's husband) has been leading the services and he does a good job. Irene and Wendy have done most of the arranging for several years now, getting speakers, music, etc.

Resort church service on the patio in back of resort house where our whole family grew up.

Chapter Sixteen: Looking Back

Right now as I am writing this in January of 2004, I can't believe that I am soon 81 years old, still very busy and involved in many ways, but especially to try to do what I can to help get our country back to the way it was, even when I was young.

In those days, even in the public schools, history, honesty, and morals were taught pretty much the way the fathers of this country believed, but now for a lot of reasons the young people in most of our public schools are being taught a lot that just isn't right. History books have been rewritten to leave out most of the true history of our forefathers. Prayer has been outlawed. Homosexuality is taught to be normal and that anything is ok if you feel or think it's ok. I will never be able to understand what has happened to our society to allow this to happen. I blame a lot of it on the ACLU (American Civil Liberties Union), Women's Lib and a lot of other things, but I put a lot of blame on the Christian world that has been silent on all of this and preachers not brave enough to speak about these things because of politics and the idea that it might offend someone.

I could go along with this if both main parties were for what's right and honest, but for the last 30 years or so, the Democratic party has voted for all the wrong things. And our judicial judges, etc. are responsible for a lot of it. The judicial system of this country really needs to be changed. It just seems they have too much power. I do have a feeling that things are getting better, and am hoping and praying that they continue to do so. Well, so much for that.

Getting back to the 1970's and our family: from the mid 1950's to past the mid 1980's, we had nine kids going through grade school and high school. I believe I have talked some of Susan and Kathy school years before; next it was Arlen. He didn't graduate from high school because he enlisted in the Army, but he did get his diploma later on. Then it was Dwight and Mike graduating in 1975 and 1976. They were both more interested in making money nailing pallets, etc. than being in sports. Then it was Patty; I don't remember too much of her high school days.

Wendy, 1965.

Then it was to Irene and my three girls. Wendy I believe started high school in 1976. She was a good student and loved to read, especially horse stories. I believe she got caught more than once in class with a horse story book on top of the book she was supposed to be reading. At that point, she was already quite involved with the horse business here at the resort. So she didn't get into sports much in high school either. She and her husband Lydell have built up the horse business so they now have 25 or more horses, and board some horses for campers or whoever.

One very special memory I have of those years when the horse business was growing is that every fall there was an overnight trail ride from Grantsburg. 150 plus horses started out at the fairgrounds, went right through downtown, then north towards Crex Meadows area a few miles and stopped for dinner. They had a chuck wagon come with the food. They then went west and wound up down by the St. Croix River and camped over night. There was always a delicious barbecued chicken supper, then some nice music and entertainment by the campfire. We had a small camper trailer we would bring up there ahead of time to sleep in and a tent, with about 5 of our kids and a few of their friends. It was rather hectic trying to get any sleep and also keeping track of the horses.

Trail ride starting in front of the cabin we built with no electric tools. The boys dug the posts, and the girls helped inside.

At that time we didn't have very many good trail horses, so by the time the kids and Irene got the more dependable horses, I ended up with a black mare, a pretty horse but really hard to handle. She just wanted to run all the time and was really hard in the mouth. The number one rule of these trail rides was to stay in line; don't pass anyone. There were two reasons I rode Inka (the mare's name): because she was the only horse left for me, and I thought I would be able to get some sense in her head, but it didn't work. She gave us a couple of nice colts but we finally traded her off, as she never did settle down.

This trail ride was from Saturday to Sunday. On Sunday morning they would have a good breakfast for us, then get everyone all saddled up ready to start out, then they would get us all in a big circle on horseback and have a short church service. I especially remember one particular trail ride. It was a rainy weekend, and especially Sunday morning, it was a steady, fairly hard rain. It is quite a picture: about 100 horses and riders (I don't think all 150 made it for the service) all in a big circle with ponchos on to keep dry and Orville the horse loving pastor in the middle on his horse leading some singing and doing the devotional. He had a poncho on (a poncho is like a rain coat with a part that goes over your head and way down and around your legs so you can keep quite dry and comfortable, especially on horseback, because the warmth from the horse's body makes you quite cozy). I will always remember Orville reading out of his Bible trying to hold it as much as possible under his poncho to keep his Bible from getting wet.

Then we would start out on the day's ride from the St. Croix River and back to Grantsburg. On this rainy morning the rest of our family chickened out, so it was just me and Wendy (maybe about 9 years old) on Dynamite and me on Inka. She was in front of me, and every once in while I would ride up beside her and say "How are you doing?", and she would look up from under her poncho and smile and say fine. I wish I could have had a picture of that.

Another fall on the Grantsburg trail ride, we all rode the whole ride. Irene always rode a white mare named Sugar Babe. She was a little older and mother to several horses. On the trail from St. Croix River to Grantsburg, Irene always wanted to be behind me. It was a beautiful trail in the woods and hills and crossing

Grandson Reid on Sugar Babe, Irene's horse.

Wood River. Going up one of these steep hills, Irene's saddle slipped so she fell off on the down side, but she still had one foot caught in the stirrup. Good old Sugar Babe just stopped, and Irene screamed for help. I couldn't get off Inka until I got to the top of that steep hill and tie her and then get back down and help Irene. I think she was still hanging with one foot in the air when I got down to her, but patient Sugar Babe was still standing right there. Irene thought it took me too long to get back to her, and let me know it. Anyway, I helped her get loose and we got straightened out and up the hill to catch up with the rest of the riders. Sugar Babe was with us for quite a few years even though she had already had several colts before we got her.

The older kids were in 4-H some years, and Irene and I were leaders for a couple years. The 4-H clubs always had a parade at the Grantsburg Fair. Each club would go in line, horses first then kids leading their calves, cows, etc. One year when Wendy was about the age of 3, she was riding on Sugar Babe as the mascot for our club. When they came in front of the grandstand, they would circle and go back. When they were just coming in front of the grandstand, Sugar Babe saw one of her offsprings up at the other end and she whined and took off on a trot to go to her and Wendy fell off. I ran in there and picked her up and caught Sugar Babe; Wendy wasn't hurt. So I put her back on and she finished the parade. I got some criticism over this but still feel it was the best for Wendy to put her back on the horse.

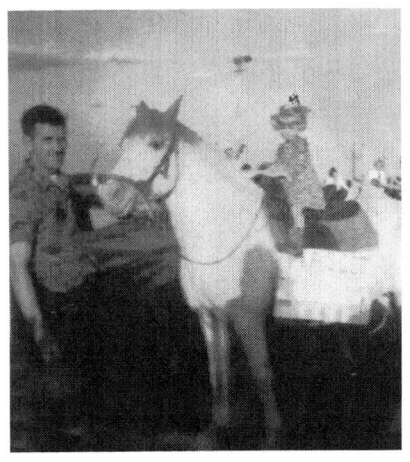

Carol with Wendy on Sugar Babe.

Wanda was born in 1965, so she and Wendy were in high school together for two years. Wanda was in volleyball and gymnastics. Frederic had a good gymnastics team and Wanda was good. So between volleyball and gymnastic meets and the other high school sports, it kept us going to games, gymnastic meets, etc. At that point I was getting quite concerned with what was happening in our schools and our country as far as a lot of things, like changing the history books to leave out a lot about our forefathers and that this nation started out as a Christian Nation. That was in the first part of the 1980's. A lot has happened since then that I will be writing about later.

I got on the school board in 1982 and was on through 1991. It was quite time consuming and it didn't seem I was able to accomplish much, but it was interesting. I went to State School Board Conventions sometimes and to the U.S School Board Convention one year. It was in Houston, Texas that year. We planned it with a vacation, first a couple days in New Orleans, then on to Texas and the convention, then down to Padre Island and a little adventure into Mexico, then back home. Wanda graduated from high school in 1983, and because I was on the school board and had a daughter graduating, I had the privilege of handing out diplomas at graduation excises. It was quite special to hand my daughter her diploma from high school.

Carol handing Wanda her
high school diploma.

Wanda with daughter Leah on Brandy
in front of horse corral in 1994.

Spirit Lake School Reunion, 1984. Around 100 students came to this very fun reunion. Third from left in front is Arlene, second from right in front is Dorothy. Behind Dorothy to the left is Bernice, behind Dorothy to the right is Pearl. Carol is far right, third row. Brother Bob is far back in middle of door. Cousin Harland Brask is two in front of Bob with white hair and glasses.

Beautiful colored leaves on the hill at the resort.
A little bit of Spirit Lake on the left side.

Chapter Seventeen: Kids Growing Up

To get back to the changes from then until now. The Civil War in the 1860's in my mind was the worst war ever. Abraham Lincoln has been a hero of mine from childhood. Lincoln and his wife Mary had ups and downs, but in my mind she was also a hero. However, when the war was over the troubles were far from over, and they still aren't over. It was a miracle that the country remained one nation under God. I believe it was because of the faith and goodness of the people both black and white and the Goverment that was able to keep the country together. From the time I was growing up even until now, there still are racial problems. It was 1963 when Rev. Martin Luther King was shot. That was a sad, bad time, but I believe from that time on things have been improving. Racism, I believe, is pretty much a thing of the past except for some trouble makers like Jesse Jackson.

In the spring of 1983, Wanda graduated from high school and in the fall Tammy started high school. Wanda was in gymnastics a couple of years, and their team went to State Competition at least one year. Then Tammy got into gymnastics as a freshman, was really good, and went to state competition all four years. Her Mom and I had to go and watch of course. This was a yearly event all four years. They were fun, exciting times.

From high school, Wanda went into Beauty School and in a couple of years she was a licensed beauty operator. Between she and her Mom being beauticians, I have never had a barbershop haircut since. I had to get back something for what it cost to get them through beauty school. Ha. Wanda worked in a beauty shop around here for awhile, but then she and a school pal decided to go east to Boston. They wanted to take all their furniture and belongings with, so Irene and I had a pickup loaded about ten feet high with all the stuff. They each had a car, so they drove too. They put a sign on the pickup, Boston or Bust. What a trip that was. It rained all the way, but we made it ok. But a lot of things got wet so they had a big job to get it all dried out and get moved into their apartment. Wanda

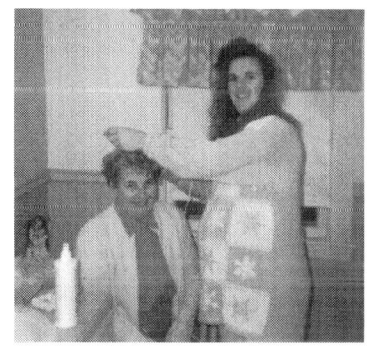

Two beauticians. Irene with Wanda.

liked it out there, fell in love with a great guy (Italian), got married and they live out there. They have three beautiful children.

We have been out to Boston a few times, I love the country because of the history. I love history, and to get out there and see some of what you learned about in school when you were young is really special. The people and the goverment have tried to conserve history in that area. Even the roads except for freeways are almost like a little improvement of what it was like in the days of Paul Revere. They are drivable but they are crooked, hilly, winding and woodsy. A lot of the residential areas do not have sidewalks in front of the houses. I love it because it gives you the feeling of the past, like in your childhood in the 1920's, etc., and also to see the beginning of our great country.

Irene, Wanda, Carol. "Boston or Bust"

But it is also very sad to see what has happened and is happening in goverment, the education system, etc., to erase the history of our forefathers and that it was mostly Christian. I am so thankful that on our money it still says In God We Trust, but the ACLU is trying hard to get that off our money and trying to erase any dependence on God out of our goverment. This is one of the biggest differences in the from then 'til now.

Back in the 1920's, 1930's, and 1940's when I was growing up there were wicked people, and a lot of basically good people who didn't express their faith much, but still had the basic moral values of being a good neighbor, being honest, trustworthy, hardworking, etc. The word trust is way too much a thing of the past. It seems most people and almost all lawyers will say you can't trust anyone, not even your family or friends. Unfortunately, this too often turns out to be so, but it shouldn't be. That is one big difference from then 'til now. Back then (unless you already had a bad name from your past or present), you were considered to be trustworthy. And a hand shake agreement meant something.

I will never forget in the 1950's one millionaire lumber man I knew. We sawed a lot of lumber for him for several years, and we bought a lot of lumber for him from the people that we sawed for. These people needed at least most of the money for the lumber right away, but Mr. Simonson had his money invested in that lumber for sometimes maybe months. We had to deliver to a railroad, and the lumber had to be graded, then hand loaded in those days into a railroad box car and shipped wherever it

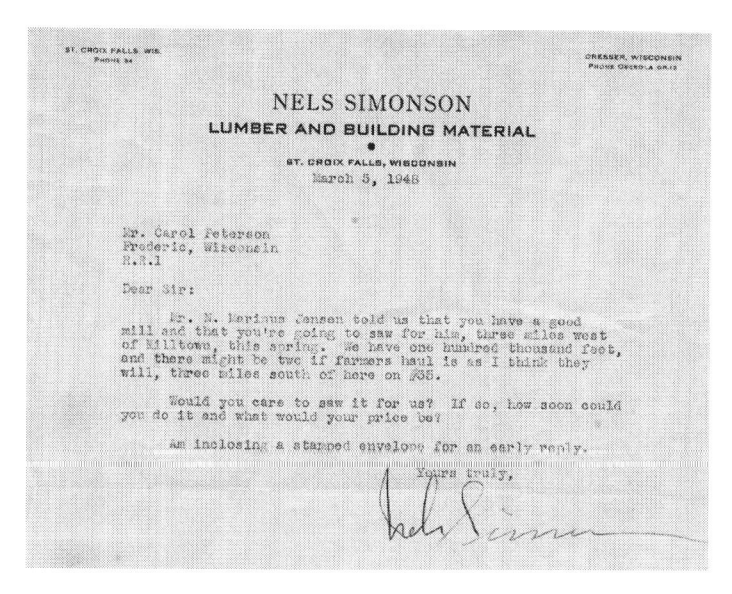

> **NELS SIMONSON**
> **LUMBER AND BUILDING MATERIAL**
>
> ST. CROIX FALLS, WISCONSIN
> March 5, 1948
>
> Mr. Carol Peterson
> Frederic, Wisconsin
> R.R.1
>
> Dear Sir:
>
> Mr. N. Marinus Jensen told us that you have a good mill and that you're going to saw for him, three miles west of Milltown, this spring. We have one hundred thousand feet, and there might be two if farmers haul is as I think they will, three miles south of here on #35.
>
> Would you care to saw it for us? If so, how soon could you do it and what would your price be?
>
> Am inclosing a stamped envelope for an early reply.
>
> Yours truly,

was going. Anyway, we would need money to pay whoever we bought the lumber from and we had to get it from Simonson.

I will never forget Simonson, he was a big guy, probably in his late sixties or early seventies. He was usually busy, but when we walked in he knew we needed money. Sometimes he didn't even say hello, he would just say "How much today, boys?", and we would say $1000.00, $2,000.00, or whatever, and he would say to his secretary "Write them out a check", then he would go on with whatever he was doing. When the check was ready he would pick it up and hand it to us and walk us to the door with a "See you later". Sometimes if he wasn't busy he would say "Come, sit down and talk". I thought he was trusting us too much with the money. So I said "Shouldn't we sign something, to make it legal?" I don't remember exactly what he said but I think it was "I trust everyone unless I find I can't trust them. You know what you've got, Grace (his secretary) knows what you've got, so we don't need more than that." I will never forget Mr. Simensen.

Back to family. In 1987, Tammy graduated from high school. Again, because I was on the school board and had a student graduating, I got to hand

ONE GRADUATE HUGGED THE SCHOOL BOARD member who handed her a diploma at the Frederic high school commencement program on May 17. Carol Peterson was the board member selected to present diplomas and shown with him is his daughter, Tammy Jo, as she receives congratulations from her father and responds in a daughterly way.

out the diplomas. This was very special for a number of reasons.
1. To hand my youngest daughter her high school diploma.
2. The looks on those kids faces as they got their diplomas and to shake their hands.
3. A feeling of satisfaction that this was kind of a graduation for us, too, because this was the last one of our kids to graduate.
4. A little feeling of uneasiness or unworthiness for me to be able to hand them their diplomas when it was something I never had.

Maybe I didn't do too badly on the school board, because the Teachers Organization each year would give a Friends Of Education plaque to one person on the school board or whoever, and in 1991 they gave that honor to me.

In the fall after Tammy graduated she went to college in the Cities for some business travel planning. She did get through that, but when she started to work, she decided that wasn't for her. After that she went to Bethel College and graduated, and there she met the man for her life.

IN APPRECIATION OF YOUR
MANY YEARS OF SUPPORT
TO OUR STUDENTS AND STAFF
OF THE
FREDERIC SCHOOL DISTRICT.
THE 1991
FRIEND OF EDUCATION
IS PRESENTED TO
CAROL PETERSON

Given this 15th day of December 1991

Wanda and Tammy 1989. Playing bookends for Wanda's father in law, a high school principal.

Reed Larson (Wendy's son), 1st Mate.

Chapter Eighteen: Sawmill Fire +

Going back to the history of the sawmill and lumber business. As I have written before, I started sawing lumber almost as soon as I got out of the Army in 1946 with my Dad's sawmill. This was also about the same time the state laws required that you had to be a registered employer if you were hiring any help. So I was a registered Wisconsin employer from I think 1949 until 1994 when we were forced out of business because of OSHA and all the new laws, etc.

From the start until 1961 we did mostly custom sawing for other people or businesses. We also bought lumber and did some logging and sawing into lumber or railroad ties, etc. on our own. So we did hire some help. We had a portable sawmill was so we could move it right into the woods where the logs were being cut, and saw it into lumber or whatever right there. The advantage was then the logs didn't need to be hauled to the sawmill and the sawdust, slab wood, etc., were left for the farmer. The slabs were good for firewood, sawdust for bedding for the animals, etc. Also, a lot of the time they were cutting lumber for a new barn, new house, etc., but the part of the lumber that had high sales value, they would sell, or we would act as a middle man and sell it for them.

This was basically the type of operation we had until in the fall of 1962 when we moved home and set up a permanent operation so as not to be portable anymore. This was really going into a new phase of our lives. First of all, we had to get set up and organized and as soon as possible start to build buildings over the mill and the place to make pallets, etc. We had to buy logs to be delivered here to saw and sell the lumber, ties, pallets, etc. to the best markets we could find. So we needed a truck and soon a semi to deliver our products to the factory, railroad treating plants, and pallets to the places that needed them, etc.

So it was a big challenge financially to pay for the logs, pay the help, pay insurance, withholding tax, etc. We did borrow some start up money, but partly

Fire at the sawmill.

because of my conservative nature and a tight banker I think we probably got about 25% of what we really needed. This basically was the problem we faced all the way from the late 1960's through the 1980's, but still

Sawmill after the fire.

the business kept growing. In the late 1970's and through 1980 we were doing up to $3 million of business a year. The resort and campground business also kept growing.

In 1971 we had a fire at the sawmill and the shop burned. This was really tough, but I did have some insurance and we did manage to buy another mill that was a little better than the one that burned and we were back in business in about two weeks.

When Arlen got out of the Army in 1975, after a few months of trying to decide what he wanted to do, he came back to Peterson Lumber full time. By that time it was starting to seem like almost too much for me to manage with the sawmill, pallets, and lumber business. Dwight was full time on the semi and Mike was busy in the pallet operation. I had gone to lumber grading school, so I was doing the lumber grading too. Arlen had management qualities, some of which he learned in the Army. After a while, I made him manager of Peterson Lumber and Wood Products. At that time we had two sawmills going, the used one I bought after the fire and one fairly automatic, smaller mill I had bought at an auction when that business quit.

At that time, there was a trend toward more automatic sawmills and machinery, and the demand for pallets, packaging material, railroad ties, and high grade lumber was great. The second hand mill was worn, and we were having a hard time getting the production we needed, as well as the ability to pay the wages, health insurance, etc.

Also, it was difficult to keep up with the demands of OSHA, a new government organization started that was supposed to make work places safer and better for the workers. Some of it was ok, but there were a lot of stupid requirements, and they hired a young inspector for our area who had no experience in the working world. He probably had a degree of some sort, but no actual experience or common sense in the working man's world.

This is another thing that has happened mostly in the last forty years. Laws might be basically good or right, but so many laws aren't written for every situation, especially with inspectors or enforcers who have no experience in that field. As an 80 year old man with about 60 years experience in the working world, I believe many laws, as well as the young inspectors, lawyers and judges have hurt the labor class more than helped it. It has made it almost impossible to stay in business, especially for small businesses. This was especially true in the wood working business. So there were a lot of the smaller operators that didn't make it.

We really needed to upgrade to be able to take care of the ever-increasing demand of the customers we had, and because we had a reputation for good quality and service. More and more factories and businesses were asking us to bid on their needs, but we needed to upgrade the sawmill and get better, specialized machinery for the pallet and skid business, and get a chipper to be able to sell our waste wood to the paper mills. An almost new, automatic sawmill came up for sale, also a debarker and chipper. We did manage to buy this equipment, but as I have written about before, we never really got the working capital we needed. So it was as hard or harder to keep the income ahead of the expenses, but that new mill was really something. It really gave us a feeling of accomplishment.

To go back to the 1970's when Arlen came back to work for Peterson Lumber; this was before we bought that new equipment. Between the sawmill, lumber business and the resort, Irene and I and the boys were all working very hard. We were all healthy and happy; the thought that we would ever fail was never in my mind.

Arlen and Vicki were renting, and wanted a place of their own. Nothing seemed available or possible to buy and he did want to build his own house anyway. In shop in high school he and one of his classmates built a model of a six sided house and that is what he wanted to build. I sold him five acres of land coming to the road from the Lundeen farm that we had bought in the early 1960's. It was just a big hill full of trees and brush, but after lots of work he did make a beautiful location out of it and then he started to build his dream, a six sided house. He got most of the

Arlen in Army uniform.

lumber from Peterson Lumber. Oh, how he worked on it, besides being full time at Peterson Lumber.

A six sided house has so many angle cuts on so much of the framing and rafters, if you make one cut at a wrong angle, you probably have to start over on another 2x4, 2x6, or whatever. Because he was full time at the mill, he was doing this mostly evenings and weekends. It did turn out to be a beautiful unique house that they (Arlen & Vicki) and all of us were very proud of! He started building it in 1977 and they moved in in 1978. Their daughter Erin was born in 1977 when they were just starting the house, and Eric was born in 1980. So they had about four good years to live in this dream house, then in 1982 it burned to the ground. This was a really sad day; they lost everything, even clothes. The neighbors were really good and gave them lots of clothes, and thankfully everyone got out safely. He did have pretty good insurance, so he soon started building a new house. He was very busy down at the mill, so he hired a contractor to do the main construction, but he did the finish work. It wasn't a six sided house, but it was beautiful with an atrium in the center. They moved into their new house in 1983, and they had some good years in it.

Arlen and Vicki's six sided house.

The sawmill pallet and lumber business kept growing all through the 1970's and 1980's and into the 1990's. But other things kept growing as well: all the problems of too much government, too many regulations as far as health insurance for your employees, and pay regulations. Increased competition in the log market and the fact that we did not have and couldn't get enough working capital made it very difficult, but we never believed in giving up and believed we were progressing and I still believe we were, if we only could have had more working capital.

Another thing that has made is difficult down through the years for a small wood & pallet business is that the company mostly has to sell to a bigger factory where lumber pallets or whatever are used for their shipping or to be remanufactured to sell to a wholesaler. The larger factories usually are better off financially, but they also take advantage of the small business and pay in 30 to 40 days or longer. This is really a problem for the small business that needs to pay his labor force weekly and his loggers cash for the logs they bring in. A lot of the time we would have $30 to $40 thousand on accounts receivable, but you need at least half of it immediately.

I made many trips to cities to pick up checks. We would call and they would promise to send it, but it seemed you couldn't depend on it. So I would ask, "Can I come in and pick up the check today?" They would sometimes say yes; then I would rush down to get it and get it in the bank to cover the Friday night checks we had to write out.

The resort and campground business kept growing, there was (and still is) a big demand for season lease spots for R.V. campers of one kind or another, but government regulations kept making it more costly and hard to comply with many stupid things. Some of the regulations do make sense, some of them don't make sense in all cases, and some don't make sense at all. The laws are made by young college graduate lawyers and politicians who really have had no hands on experience with the businesses they are impacting.

Anyway, we struggled along until in the 1990's we were forced into Chapter 11 Bankruptcy by a lawyer who I guess helped us some. This was quite a heart breaking and hard time for us. We had to lay off our workers and shut the mill down and all the machinery and equipment was sold at auction. I had been to some sawmill woodworking bankruptcy auctions because you sometimes could get a good price on equipment that we needed. So part of our equipment was from failing sawmill or woodworking businesses. This was always kind of a sad feeling for me, but it never entered my mind that it would happen to us, but it did.

The day of the auction it rained all day. I felt so bad and sick that I never went out of the house all day; I just cried! Arlen was there, but Dwight and Mike were already working at other jobs. We don't how much the rain hurt the auction, but it didn't come out as well as we hoped. So there was still much debt against the resort. Our bankruptcy lawyer was supposedly negotiating a settlement with our bank so that we could keep the resort, but it seemed they were getting nowhere. I didn't know then, but I have learned since that bankruptcy lawyers don't want you to talk to anyone about the case.

I knew the man handling the case for the bank a little bit, so I finally confronted my lawyer, asking him why I couldn't go and talk to this man at the bank and he said, "I don't want you to, but I can't stop you and besides we don't seem to be getting anywhere. So if you want to, go ahead." Irene and I made an appointment with him and talked about it. We never actually talked figures that day but he seemed very friendly and compassionate to us. After a few days we got a letter and an offer of settlement that really was better than we had dared to hope. So now if we could just make the payments, we wouldn't lose the resort. Wendy & Lydell were considering buying the resort, but they were really already too involved to take on that much more. Anyway with them and some help from Wanda and Dana, we managed to pay the payments.

Our 25th Anniversary.
L-R: Carol's sister Pearl, Irene, Carol, Irene's brother Leroy.

Dwight with grandson Carson.

Back L-R: Bob Dahl (sister Florence's husband) holding grandson Noah Wright, Elisha Wright, Carol. Front L-R: Isabelle and Paige Burton.

Irene and Arlen with Wanda and Wendy, early 1970's.

Ross Larson (Susan's son), in his element.

Arlen with his daughter, Naomi.

Arlen with Naomi's children.

Family 1985. Back L-R: Carol, Bob, Gladys, Florence, Arlene.
2nd Row L-R: Gene, Carole, Linda. Front: Bernice.

Carol with great-grandson Carson.

Irene with grand-daughter Leah (Wanda's daughter).

Great-grandson Carson and grandson Evan (Wanda's son).

Chapter Nineteen: Selling to Dwight and Nancy

Dwight and Nancy were getting interested in possibly buying the resort. Dwight had a heart for the place because it was home to him and he had memories of the good times he had in the summer with a lot of the camper kids that came back year after year. Dwight and Nancy both had good jobs in Luck. Dwight sold his beautiful river house that he had worked so hard on; it was a beautiful place with the upper Trade River running around two sides of it. I could write volumes just about that place. Nancy also had a neat trailer home in Frederic.

It was March 7, 2000 when Dwight and Nancy made a land contract to buy Birchwood Beach. They helped us a lot before that time, and we have helped them all we could since that time.

This deal probably would have happened sooner except for one thing: Dwight didn't think he could live in that big old house, even though Irene and I and a lot of people thought it was a beautiful place. We had put so much work into it with help from my Dad and Ardelle's Dad. I have so many memories of those two working together. From childhood to becoming an adult, I thought there was nothing my Dad couldn't do and do it good and right. I still believe that, but by now I realize he maybe wasn't as 100% perfect as I thought he was. He built a new house on the home place the year I got out of the Army. He must have been planning that new house in his mind for years, because all the lumber was from the woods at home cut into logs and sawed into lumber on his own sawmill. I'm sure I even helped with some of it before I went in the Army.

My Dad truly was an expert on ability and memory. I have never known anyone that could come close to him at being able to find the right board for every job and be able to fit it in perfect. As far as memory, when he got the house built he could say: "Remember that oak tree that was back by the pond down towards the lake? That window sill (or whatever) was

Family room in the old resort house.

from the lumber of that tree."

Anyway, to get back to Herman (Ardelle's Dad) and Dad helping on our house. Herman had worked in sales; selling cars or whatever, but in his later years he did want to do more woodwork. So it was really fun to see the two of them work together, and the lumber they were using was what I had sawed. In the den, we had hardwood paneling mixed with all kinds of hardwood (ash, oak, maple, birch, butternut, hickory, cherry, and maybe more). It really was beautiful. There were two or three other major changes in the house when Irene and I got married and we had to have more room. Then in about 1985, we did the last major change on the house: an open stairway and a loft with beam ceiling, etc. We liked it a lot, so it was pretty hard to give it up with all the memories, etc.

Open staircase in old resort house.

Dwight and Nancy were trying hard to figure out what to do, but no location on the resort was as good as where the old house was to run the resort from. In the winter of 2000, they finally decided they could live in the old house for a while. This was great news, but also meant Irene and I would have to move! For years I had been looking at a spot up on the hill across from the resort and to the one side of the old sawmill buildings. I had thought for years it would be a great place for our so called retirement.

It is a beautiful spot with a view of the lake and the resort and somewhat in the middle with a view of four of our kids' homes. That part just happened; it wasn't planned. Mike is in the remodeled old schoolhouse to the left; Dwight and Nancy on the resort; to the right and southeast is Lydell & Wendy's place. They bought land from our best neighbor, Bob Hinrichs, and built a new house and barn for the horse business. Then about 200 yards south is Tammy & Phil's new double wide. They also bought land from Bob Hinrichs. Their land borders ours (the old mill acres). Their kids, our grandkids, can in five minutes or less run across the field to our house. Wendy & Lydell usually have some horses in the pasture area, which is

View of the sawmill from our house.

another plus for us because we like horses.

There is no place in the world I would rather live than here! There are so many memories of the eight years in Spirit Lake School in the 1930's, as well as after we bought what there was of the resort in 1955. The good times of all the good and bad times through the years. The good times of family, our kids being born and growing up here and all the years when we all worked so hard to scratch out a living and to make it a more beautiful and nice place to come to. This was our hope and love for Birchwood Beach Campgrounds. As my Dad said to our neighbor so many years ago, God expects us to make the earth a more beautiful place than before we came into it.

To get back to March of 2000, Dwight and Nancy had decided they could live in the house at least for a while. So Irene and I had to move. We already had the location up on the hill above the mill buildings, part of the mill land which was now ours free and clear, but we needed a house. To build from scratch would have been my first choice but time made this out of the question. Irene always thought she liked mobile homes, the double wides.

So we went house hunting; this was quite an experience. These pre-built houses really are nice, there is so much choice, and the dealers really are competitive for your business. After a lot of looking, we decided on the house we are currently in. It has a lot of windows, we liked the floor plan and the appearance from the side facing the road.

So now to get the site ready. It took a little bulldozing to level the site and then pour a slab of cement to put it on. We decided that we old people didn't need a basement, and besides we didn't have time to put one in. Both halves of the house came on the same day. The next day about six men came and put the two together, sealed it up, finished the roof, and would you believe that by night it was all ready to move into. It was really something.

Moving our new house in.

We had a new well drilled already, and the sewer project was done. Here is another difference from then 'til now: then you could dig or drive your own well and put a hand pump on it, then build an outhouse or figure out your own sewer system. Now you have to get permits and so called specialists to figure out what you need or can do. Then the work has to be done by licensed people. Some of it is good, and some of it is stupid.

Living room at the new house.

We moved in on Memorial weekend, 2000. What a job to figure out what to do with 50 years of accumulation! Luckily, we had the mill sheds to store stuff in while we decided what we wanted in the new house, what to save and what to get rid of. Now we were happily living in our new home!

This was really something for me. I have always enjoyed building, remodeling, etc. To move into a new home that wasn't here a couple days ago and have all the conveniences, beauty, etc. (at least inside) of a modern home was amazing. It sure is a big change from what was possible less than 100 years ago. One thing I do miss is firing and heating with wood. In my mind there is no kind of heat that compares to wood heat. If I live long enough, I hope to build a building with a lot of memories and a wood stove. Ha.

I have written about some of the years of the late 1970's to 2000, but those years were busy with both good things and bad things that I can't seem to remember much more that I haven't already written about.

The technology in every way has advanced so much in the last 50 years or so. It is really more than my old mind can grasp. To me, much of it is almost like a miracle. Some of it is good, some of it in my opinion is bad. One thing I think is bad about this computer age is that kids and adults get so used to using the computer that without it they can't do anything. I think the educational system is partly to blame. When I was on the school board I tried to get them to not let any of the kids below a decided age use calculators or computers to do their math. Give them tests to make sure they could do it the old fashioned way. To me its really disgusting when 90% of the population can't or won't do any math without an electric calculator to use. instead of using their head.

In my school days here in good old Spirit Lake School

the teacher would plan math competition races for speed and accuracy and they were a lot of fun. Of course in those days there was no TV to watch or games to play on the computer, etc., but what we had was good, honest hard work and fun. We did play ball; we pooled our pennies until we could afford to buy a soft ball. We managed not to lose it, and someone would sew it together when it started to come apart. We also played games like hide and seek , and games like Flying Dutchman, Pump Pump Pull Away, etc. I don't remember ever feeling bored or sorry for ourselves. Some families were poorer than others, but for the most part there seemed to be such a neighborhood bond to help each other. My memory is mostly of love and concern and not hate. It wasn't always perfect, but except for tragedy like Mother dying, Loretta dying, etc., the memories are really good.

Our family, 2001.

Irene on the steps of the old resort house.

Flowers in a little wagon rescued from a trash pile out at Wanda and Dana's, near Boston.

Irene with Tammy and Phil's children, Paige, Isabelle, and Jenna in the above-ground pool by our new house.

Sunrise through our living room window. Unbelievable beauty.

Chapter Twenty: Irene's Heart Attack

To get back to the 1990's to 2000 and on. In 1991, Irene wasn't feeling very well, so her doctor decided she needed to have an angiogram. So we went down to Abbott Northwestern and she had the angiogram and it turned out one artery was quite plugged. We could have gone home and made a later appointment to have an angioplasty done (this is a ballon system they used more then than they do now), but they thought it needed to be as soon as possible. They said they could do it that day if it would work out for us. So we made a fast decision and decided we had better do it. It was quite an anxious time for us, but she come through it well. She had to stay in the hospital for two days. I stayed down there too. She was pretty sick so I don't know what she was thinking, but for me it was really a time of praying and thinking about what could happen. But she recovered fast, and soon was her old self until the year 2000 when she had a heart attack.

Those last years of the 1900's, there was a lot of anxiety about possible terrorism and the concern that 2000 was going to be the end of the world. One of the big fears was that we would lose our electric power which we are so dependent upon. So the demand for electric generators of all sizes for homes, business etc. I suppose this was good for the companies selling generators. We had bought a big one years before for fear of tornados causing power failure, so we were ok. The tension of wondering what the year would bring I believe was on everyone's mind, but the year 2000 came in as peacefully as every other year before.

I don't really think these tensions had anything to do with Irene's heart attack, but on January 1, 2000 Irene got severe pains in her heart, so we went to Grantsburg as fast as we could. They checked her out and decided she better get down to Abbott Northwestern right now. So they called in a helicopter, and before I knew it she was off in the helicopter. This gave me a helpless feeling I had never known before. Then I had to head home and get

Carol and Irene, 2000.

some things and head down to the hospital.

Of course, she got there before I did, but she hadn't gone into surgery yet. So it was a waiting experience until she went in for surgery and then another waiting time to see it over with. In the meantime, Wanda must have jumped on a plane from Boston. Our granddaughter Sarah picked her up at the airport and brought her to the hospital. I'm not sure, but I think she was there before Irene went in for surgery.

I don't know what all went through my mind, but I kind of remember thinking back about Ardelle and wondering and praying that I wouldn't lose Irene too. Anyway, they finally wheeled her into the operating room. Then the suspense for about three hours until she was back in the recovery room seemed forever, but I did get a lot of support from all of our daughters. Patty, Tammy or Dwight must have called Wanda about her mother; that is something that could not have happened 100 years ago.

Irene seemed to have come through everything ok and was coming along well for a few hours, then they discovered her heart cavity was filling up with blood. The nurses were frantic. The surgeon who operated on her just happened to come to see how she was doing, found out what was happening, and realized something had to be done within seconds. He poked something right down through her chest into the heart cavity to relieve the pressure. He explained to me and Wanda that if he hadn't poked down through her chest she would have been gone in minutes, but thank God he came just then.

So then she was again on the road to recovery. They had her in intensive care for a couple of days then moved her into recovery for five more days. So she was there seven nights total. I stayed right there and slept in the visitor's waiting room. You weren't really supposed to stay there overnight, but we did and they put up with us. I say we because Wanda stayed with me about three nights until she had to go home to her family. Patty then stayed with me one night; we kept going in and checking on her every little while day and night until she went home.

She seemed to be recovering nicely for a week or more. Then she ended up with a lot of chest pains so I called the hospital and they said rush her in. So I did and they decided she'd better get back down to Abbott Northwestern quickly, so she got another helicopter ride. This time I think Tammy went with me down there. It seemed they were having a hard time knowing what was going on, but she was never scheduled for more surgery. They kept her for about a week, and she kept getting better. They never really told us, but it kind of leaked out that they had given her the wrong medicine when we went home the first time, They never did explain this to us but we never got a bill for any of the last time, not even for the helicopter ride. Then she improved fast and she was her old self again.

The summer of 2000 we were both busy on the resort and getting ground work, etc. done on our new home, and we needed a garage and workshop. Some of Dwight's in-laws lived up by Hayward, Wisconsin and knew of a resort that was being demolished to make room for condominiums. There was a really good garage that we got very cheap, but we had to take it down and bring it home in sections. We really worked hard that day. We got it all down and loaded up on Dwight's truck and machine trailer and on my pickup and brought it home in one day. That was a day I will always remember.

We unloaded everything close to where we intended to build the garage, but that's as far as it got until the summer and fall of 2001. Irene kept doing fine, so in the winter of 2001 we went to Branson to be with my Army buddy and his wife which we had done several times before. We had a good time down there and were headed for New Windsor, Illinois to visit my cousin Bert Larson and his wife Maxine, which we usually did when we came from Branson. Irene was feeling really good, but in the night she started to have chest pain that wouldn't go away. In the early morning she took a nitroglycerin of Bert's and it didn't help, so Maxine and I took her to the clinic they went to and they thought it was probably another heart attack coming on. There is a heart hospital in Davenport, Iowa, which was only about 35 miles away. So she went by ambulance, went into surgery and they put in one more stent; she had 3 put in the first time at Abbott Northwestern the winter before. About three or four days later they let her go home and she recovered fast. Then in April, 2001 she was out helping Elise cleaning cabins and fell off a chair and broke her wrist. So she was one handed for a while, but that didn't slow her up much.

Carol and Irene on the scaffolding with their helpers, building the garage.

Then finally that summer we did put the garage up. Dwight

helped to get the cement poured for the foundation and floor, but then Irene and I put the walls up with no help. We made it 24X30 so it took 3 more rafters and a few more 2X4s in the walls. When we got done, there was hardly a piece of 2x4 or lumber left. This gave us two old people a great feeling of accomplishment.

Carol with sister Pearl, 2001.

Before we knew it, it was Christmas again and New Years, 2002. I couldn't believe it; here I am 79 years old and still in pretty good shape. We went to Branson again; I guess this was the last time my sister Pearl went with us. Along toward spring Irene had some problems, so on the 31st of May she had a hysterectomy and there was some cancer, so she had to have 29 radiation treatments. We had to go five days a week, with the weekend off. We went back and forth so I could be at home, so somebody took her down every day. It must have done a good job because when she was checked, there was no cancer.

So she was her old self again, until in March of 2003, we had some good weather, so the snow was gone except for some ridges of ice. We had gotten two or three inches of loose, light snow, so you couldn't see where the ridges were, making it very slippery. I wasn't feeling well that day, so she said "I'll go get the mail,." I said "OK, but be careful; it's really slippery in spots." It's always seemed to me that women (especially Irene) never were as surefooted as men. And Irene has always had another problem. I don't think the Lord made her with a slow speed, she always is in high gear.

She went down the hill and when I looked out the window there she was sitting in the snow. I didn't get excited right away because I didn't think she was hurt, but about that time Corey (Dwight's son) just drove in and stopped by her to see what happened. She said "I think I broke my foot." He lifted her in his rig and brought her up to the house. Then I brought her to the hospital. So she was in a wheel chair or walker a good part of the summer, but that didn't stop her from helping Elise in the cabins, etc. She's almost as good as new now.

Chapter Twenty-One: Irene's Own Words

Irene is going to write in her own words some of her thoughts and feelings through these times.

I brought 2000 in with a bad heart attack!
We had been over to Pine City shopping and ate out and when we got home , I was putting things away and all of sudden I didn't feel good, it seemed like someone was standing on my chest, so I told Carol I was going to lay down. Then soon I felt pain going down both of my arms. I told Carol and he called 911. The ambulance came and took me to Grantsburg; they got me stable and ready for the helicopter ride to Abbott Northwestern. I had always thought it would be fun to ride in one of those things when they would fly by, but I was so sick I don't remember much. I remember them lifting off the oxygen mask and asking if I was ok. I don't remember how long before I went in for surgery, but I guess I gave them a scare. They put in three stents and my family was wonderful. I came home in one week and then I had to go to Grantsburg for rehabilitation.

After two weeks I woke up with chest pains. I took nitroglycerin, but it didn't help and I thought, man, here we go again. Will I make it this time? I think my strong faith kept me from panic. I just placed myself in God's hands and believed however it went would be God's will. From there on I was so sick I don't remember much at all. One morning I woke Carol at about 4:30 AM and he called and took me in to the hospital at Grantsburg (my rehab gal had told me if I ever had chest pains to get to the hospital right away). They couldn't figure it out, so they sent me again by helicopter back to Abbott Northwestern where they did a lot of testing. They didn't tell me anything, but I asked my nurse and she said it was from one of the pills I was taking, that was a side effect and they knew it, so they had taken me off of it. I was there almost a week in

Irene with a grandchild, 1980's.

February, 2000. I recovered fast and got back to the excitement of shopping and moving into a new house. Wanda and Dana and kids and Kathy came from the east and west to help me decorate, arrange furniture etc. Then also helping at the resort, it was a summer to remember.

In the winter of 2001 we went to Branson to meet Carol's buddy and his wife and on our way back we stopped to see Carol's cousin Bert and Maxine Larson and in the night I had some chest pains and so I got up and Bert gave me his nitroglycerin pills and I tried that and it didn't help so Maxine and Carol took me to there clinic and they checked me and thought it was my heart so they sent me by ambulance to Davenport, Iowa and they put in one stent and I was there from Tuesday to Saturday before they let me go home. This was in the beginning of March.

In April I was helping clean and get cabins ready with Elsie. She went to her trailer to get something; I was up on a chair getting dishes down to wash and I fell off and broke my right wrist. So Carol took me to Grantsburg and they x-rayed it and there was no one to set it there so they sent me to Cambridge to get it done. What an ordeal. It is hard doing things with one hand. Carol did a lot of the cooking and helping me. He was great....

Then in April I had some signs that things weren't right. I went to my doctor and they set me up with Dr. Flom, but I couldn't get with her for a few days. When I saw her, she took a sample and about a week or so later she called me and said "You have cancer." Oh, what a shock. "It is 60% in your uterus, so we need to do a hysterectomy." What a blow, one never wants to hear that word.

So I went back to Abbott Northwestern and had the hysterectomy. It was quite a painful recovery after I got home, then after six weeks I had to go for radiation treatments at Abbott Northwestern for 29 treatments, Monday through Friday with weekends off. The actual treatments only took about ten minutes, but it

Carol and Irene, 2000.

took one and half hours to get there, and the same going back. We went back and forth and different people took turns taking me too. Carol did it the most, and also Elsie, LeRoy (my brother) Wanda, Tammy, and Patty. I would get tired but other than that it wasn't bad. It was just a precaution to be sure it was all gone. She figured she got it all. Then I would go for a check up in 3 months, then another 3 months, then 6 months. And 6 months is due now in 2004.

Then on March 4th my brother and I went over to my sister Lucille's for dinner for her birthday. Carol didn't feel well so he didn't go. We had a good trip and when we got back Carol hadn't gone to get the mail, so I said I would. I went to get it, and there was some ice and a light coat of snow over it and I slipped and fell and broke my left ankle. Corey had just come and was talking to Carol and looked out and saw me sitting in the snow at the turn by the mill sheds. So Corey came down and helped me into his rig and brought me up to the house. Carol came out and Corey said just take my rig and I'll call and tell them you're coming. So to Grantsburg again. They x-rayed it and it was broken bad. The bone doctor was coming the next day so they put me in the hospital, they wrapped it and put it on a pillow. So the next day they put a cast on and I had to stay for a few days. When I came home I had to get around with a walker or a wheel chair.

I know with all of these health problems that God was with me and a lot of people were praying for me. I really have a wonderful family and friends. Carol was the best... At this writing we are a clan of 50 or more family, husbands, wives, grandchildren, and great grandchildren.

Whole Family at Wanda's wedding.

Our Patty and her cousin Jackie Peterson on a family canoe trip, 1970's.

Wendy and Lydell on their wedding day.

Frederic Family Days, 1988.

Irene's flowers in our front yard.

With the grandchildren.

Irene, Carol, Paige, Mark, Devyn, Leah, Isabelle.

Carol, Irene, granddaughter Holly's twins, Devyn, Tammy's daughters Paige and Isabelle.

Chapter Twenty-Two: Our New House

In the year 2000 when we got our new house and moved in, Dwight and Nancy moved into the resort house. That house is really where we raised our family. This of course made it a very special place with all kinds of memories. Sybil lived with us for 20 years or more. We were between 7 and 10 people living there for many years. To make enough bedrooms, for a few years I made the living room into two bedrooms with a hall going through to the family room, but it really went pretty well. Through the years we kept making improvements, so it really was quite nice.

From the lake and the road it looked big and beautiful. There was a lot of beautiful paneling from all kinds of trees. I hardly ever bought any lumber, it was from the mill, oak, ash, maple, cherry, butternut, elm, aspen, most of the species that were in the house One thing there were bats in that house all the years. It seemed we never could get them all. To me knocking down a bat flying around the house was kind of a challenge or almost fun, but nobody else saw it that way, especially Nancy or Irene or the girls. There were other things about that house that were not the best, but it was home.

Dwight and Nancy made some improvements to make it nicer for them, until they could get a new house. In the later part of the summer of 2003 it was scheduled to happen. They moved into one of the cabins and we started to salvage as much as we could of that beautiful paneling and the ceiling deck and open rafters in the newest remolded part over the dinette and office and entrance part. Being able to salvage this much made it easier for me to give up the place and start dreaming in my head of the memory house we are hoping to be able to build.

The poor old house looked pretty sick after all this salvaging, so now it was ready to be knocked down. It was knocked down with a backhoe. The same machine dug a big hole across the road to haul the knocked down house into and then

Salvaging from the old resort house.

Tear down and wreckage of the old resort house.

burn it. It really made a big pile and really a big fire the day we burned it. We had decided we didn't dare burn until there was snow on the ground or in a heavy rain. This was in October; one day it was pouring down rain, so Dwight and I decided if we could get it started, this was a good time to burn it. There were a lot of different kinds of hardwoods and softwoods, so when it got started it really burned hard, flames 40-50 feet in the air in spite of the pouring down rain. It really burned up good except for some that was over the edges of the hole. When they dug the hole they put all the dirt in a big pile to one end of the hole.

To go back a little in this story, for years when we were building up the sawmill area and the resort, I had a smaller bulldozer which was really the heart of a lot of projects, but it was sold at the sale. Now with our new house, there is a lot of yard improvement work and work in the mill yard to make it look better, as well as possible uses for the resort on projects that never seem to end. Even at 80+ years old, I still enjoy getting on the bulldozer and doing the earth moving jobs. Anyway, I was keeping my eyes open for an older bulldozer that I could afford and I had just found one in the summer of 2003: a John Deere 440 in really good shape at a fair price. I had just bought it a little before the house came down.

After the big burning, it was my job to push in whatever was around the edge of the hole, let it burn up, and then push the big pile of dirt back in the hole and level it off. I was really surprised at how few ashes there were from that big house.

Carol on his 1962 bulldozer.

Covering up that hole with the ashes from the house, going forth and back with the bulldozer, gave me a lot time to think. I was smiling, but sometimes the tears would almost come.

Another highlight of the spring of 2003 was getting a maple syrup evaporator for processing the sap from the maple trees into maple syrup. From the time I was just a kid at home we always tapped the maple trees in the spring and cooked maple syrup by just boiling the sap in big flat pan down to syrup. It takes 30 to 40 gallons of sap to make a gallon of syrup. When we bought Birchwood Beach in 1955, there were a lot of big beautiful maple trees in the hills of the upper campground. So it was a family project (but I guess mostly mine) to tap the trees, gather the sap and cook it to maple syrup. What a job, but it was always exciting to see the sap dripping out of the tree into a pail, and then when you were cooking to see it gradually change from the water like sweet sap to real pure maple syrup.

I will always remember one night Dwight, about 8 years old, and I were sitting by the fire, keeping it going while cooking syrup. Dwight must have been thinking about the whole concept of making maple syrup; he said "I can't think of anything else but maple syrup that you don't have to add anything else to it, you only cook the water out of the sap. That's why it is pure maple syrup." I had never really thought about that before. I guess that was the young teaching the old.

As the years went by, easier methods of making maple syrup were developed. An evaporator makes the sap goes slower into tubs with the heat of the fire around the tubes, and it keeps feeding through until when it gets through the other end it is syrup. This is so much faster than the old way.

Now it is March, 2004 and it's just about time for maple syrup season to begin. You may wonder why the sap only runs this time of year. This is because when the sap comes up out of the ground through the trunk of the tree to the branches to make the leaves, there is so much more sap than is needed to make the leaves, so the extra just drops to the ground. So when you tap the trunk of the tree you are just getting a small portion of the extra sap the tree is producing, and it doesn't hurt the tree at all.

For years I dreamed of having an evaporator, and now at 80 years

Carol, Irene, son-in-law Phil holding Jenna, son-in-law Lydell. By the maple syrup evaporator.

old I have one. It is exciting. It is still a lot of work, but it is fun, and we have maple syrup on the table all the time. I never get tired of it. As far as the work I now have son-in-laws, sons, daughters, grandchildren, and great grandchildren to help, and most of them love it like I do. So we do it for fun and to be around the whole extended family. We do also sell a little. Another thing that's fun about it is that it comes from the sap of the maple trees right in the Season Lease Campground.

Old resort house, coming down.

Dwight and Nancy's new house, almost finished.

Just for fun, about 1983.

Tapping the maple trees for maple syrup. Phil with Paige and Isabelle.

Chapter Twenty-Three: Politics

March 8-2004

I am finally getting to the now times of from then 'til now. There are many of the changes and memories of the then times I have forgotten to write about. But now to go back to the preface and what I said there. I still think and hope and pray that more people are thinking about what has happened to faith in God and our morals but I think we need to do more than think and pray about it. We have to put feet on our prayers. Talk about it in our homes, in our churches wherever we are.

I really believe that this next presidential election is the most important presidential election there has ever been since the Civil War and President Abraham Lincoln, or the end of the Revolutionary War and George Washington and the great men that helped form our country.

I really believe this coming election is not just a contest between Democrats and Republicans. It is a battle between Good and Evil. I am sure this statement will upset a lot of Democrats, but I can't see it any other way. In November of 2003, I put a letter to the editor in our local paper which I think says what I believe, so I am going to put it in here.

Democrats and Republicans

I believe in the two party system. Otherwise government could become more like a dictatorship, but ever since President Reagan and before, the Democratic Party has been gradually straying from God and the Bible, which was the cornerstone our forefathers built this country on. I could quote many statements from the founding fathers to support this and I believe that is why this country has been blessed like it has. To me it is rally sad what has happened.

God has been taken out of our schools, history books have been changed to hardly mention the forefathers and what they stood for. Sex and abortion have really gotten out of hand. Any mention of God in government is being stomped out. Homosexuality and much more that is wrong has become part of our life.

Who is to blame? Many: The ACLU, the media, Hollywood, our former President and his wife, our judical system (Supreme

Court) and Christians (Democrats and Republicans) who have remained silent rather than speaking out. But mainly the Democratic Party for going along with and promoting these things that are wrong.

Right now the Democrats are doing all they can to ruin President Bush. Lies upon lies or whatever it takes to hopefully get the Democrats back in power.

It is really hard for me the way the Democrats and the media want to blame Bush for everything. Have you (they) forgotten Sept 11? Should we not try to stop terrorism? To me, Democrats in power and to some extent the media have somewhat the attitude of Saddam Hussein that human life is not important unless it hurts me or mine.

Saddam Hussein was much like Hitler, who didn't put value on human life. I was in Germany in WW2 and in the Army Occupation and learned from the people how Hitler misled them.

I really believe we have a President and his wife, Laura, Vice President Cheney, Condoleeza Rice, Colin Powell and all the good people working for the good of the U.S. and the world like there hasn't been since maybe Abraham Lincoln's day. I really believe most Democrats are good people and if it had been up to them, many things adopted by the Democratic Party would not have had your vote.

My hope for you Democrats is that in the next election you would vote Republican, then get back to your Democratic Party and straighten it up for what's right and honest.

If you disagree with this, check the voting records in Congress and you will find it was and is the Liberals in Congress who voted on issues to please the desires of the Entertainment World, and our former President and his wife who led us away from the belief in our forefathers who really believed One Nation Under God.

I think one reason the Liberal Party thinks we have to get rid of any mention of the Christian heritage is because there are so many Islams and other so called religious people in our country, and more coming in all the time. Also, the Atheists want to get rid of any mention of God in our government. This is a problem because our Constitution says freedom of religion, but it doesn't say freedom from religion. That is a problem of interpretation that is wrong.

I believe we should be teaching our children the true history of our country and that it was founded as a Christian Nation. If the atheists, Islamic people, and other so called religious people want to live in our great country and gain citizenship here, they can believe what they want to, but we should still in our schools teach true History and not omit any of it. I would like to see all of our students have to pass an American History test that included from the Revolutionary War through World War II. This should include private school students as well. This of course is my thinking but will most likely never happen.

Another thing is the United Nations. In the past, I think the United Nations did some good, but now they are for world government and it seems the Liberals go along with this. I sincerely hope and pray this never happens or this is definitely the beginning of the end.

Another problem I have is the complacency of Christians. If I try to talk about the problems in our government to Christians, the answer I get so many times is "Don't worry, the Lord is in control; we don't have to worry or do anything." So they don't. I believe this is wrong. I believe like my Dad we are in this world to try to make it a better place. It seems to me too much of the Christian's attitude is somewhat like the Good Samaritan story: walk to the other side of the road, I don't want to be bothered with it. I really believe if we want this country to continue to be the great country it has been, Christians have to get involved in the affairs of their country.

It is several years since I first got the idea of this book, from then 'til now, and started it. Sometimes for months or years it just got side tracked but now with Irene's help and my sister Dorothy's daughter Janice, we hope to go to print. It is now September, 2004.

At the start of writing from then 'til now, my idea was to hopefully get the younger people to see what life was like in this country 60 to 100 years ago and the great progress there has been. I hope to help them appreciate it and not complain, but try to do their part to make it a better country, as well as a better local community where they live.

One of the big changes from then till now, especially in the last 30 years, maybe even more so in the last 10 years or so is in the computers and video field. It is just unbelievable for me, but it even seems to be for those who are educated in this field. I am sure there has been some good in all this, but when the computer age was just starting some years ago I used to call it the Devil's tool, and I'm still not too sure about this.

The other biggest change from then 'til now is in the moral attitude in our country. What is being taught in our universities, colleges, high schools, grade schools, and even kindergarten I believe is much to blame. It is really too bad, but I hope and pray that with God's help, Christians getting involved, and good things shaking the entertainment world like the movie "Passion of the Christ" has, I believe and hope and pray that the years ahead will get better. So I'm going to end this by repeating the last paragraph of the preface.

    I feel there is a trend now of thinking seriously about God and morals, hard work, etc., and there will have to be if this world is going to last. So I'm dedicating this to my nine kids and all my grandchildren and great grandchildren and to anyone who reads it. May it help them see what a change has taken place in the 1900's, and I hope it might help on the road of life, plus hopefully provide some enjoyment.

Carol and Irene, Winter 2004.

Chapter Twenty-Four: Reminiscing

The last writing was March 8, 2004; now it is September 15, 2004 and we still have not gone to print, but we think we are getting very close. So much has happened in the last six months, and so much has gone through my mind about From Then 'Til Now that I forgot about. So I want to add a little more about the changes in the working world.

I was talking to a farmer a few days ago about modern harvesting machines now compared to what we had in the 1930's. We were talking mostly about the corn harvest; one thing that hasn't changed is Mother Nature. There are perhaps better predictions now than there were then, but you still can't be sure ahead of time if the corn will ripen for a good crop to be harvested for the ear corn and the cornstalks left to be chopped up for fertilizer or baled or whatever. Or if it isn't going to ripen, the decision needs to be made to cut it and chop it up for silage. This decision was much the same back in the 1930's, except there was a definite need for the ear corn for feed for the pigs, chickens, etc., and the rest was used for silage.

Just at the right time when it was sure the ears were almost mature, here is what we did. In the 1930's, most corn, potatoes, etc. were planted in 3 foot apart rows to be able to cultivate and also the corn binders were made to work best in 3 foot rows. Now I think it is mostly 18 inch rows and the harvest machine takes several rows at a time. They don't cultivate much, just use weed killer instead and lots of commercial fertilizer to make it really grow. I don't know if farmers were stupid in those days, but I don't think so. For one thing, commercial fertilizer was just starting to be available in the 1930's, and it was so expensive that most farmers couldn't afford it. The only fertilizer was manure from the animals.

So to get the best value from your crop to fill the needs for the winter for your cows, pigs, and chickens, this is how we harvested the corn. Just at the right time we would do what we called snap corn. Usually there would be at least two people doing this (probably ten years or older). Each person would take two rows and snap the ears off and drop them in the designated row of the four rows. The next step is to cut the corn with the corn binder pulled with three horses. Then we would load the corn bundles by hand and haul it into the silo by the barn, unload the corn into a silo filler which chopped the stalks short and blew it up into the silo. Usually there were one or two people in the silo tramping the corn down and handling the distribution pipe. This was a neighborhood operation, with four to five teams and wagons hauling corn into the silo filler. So usually it was one day at a place until all the silos were filled.

Then after the corn bundles were hauled off the field, it was time for those rows of corn ears that were in every fourth row, 12 feet apart. We drove the horses and wagon between these rows, husked the corn, left the husks in the field, and hauled the husked corn to the corn crib.

Today, it is done one of two ways, either cut and chopped into wagons and blown into some kind of silo, or it is left to really mature. In the second case, they go out with a picker/sheller, and it goes into storage all in one operation.

What a difference it was from then until now. There are two main reasons for the differences. 1) New and better harvesting machines are continually being invented and made. 2) Back in the 1930's, wages were $1.00 a day and there still weren't enough jobs, so almost everyone was poor. It was a matter of surviving, but I didn't realize it. Every day was exciting, and when night came I was always thinking about the next day. I remember my Dad when I asked what we would be working on the next day, would say "Can't you wait until morning, and then we'll see?"

This got to be long about corn and farming, but I think it really shows the changes from then until now. It was much the same in the timber, logging, and sawmill business. My first experience cutting logs was with my Dad and a two man cross-cut saw. Then in the late 1940's or early 1950's my partner and I bought our first chain saw, a 10 HP Mercury. It weighed over 100 pounds. It would really cut, but it wasn't very dependable. It cost about $900.00. Now you can buy a good chain saw for around $300.00 that weigh about 20 pounds. What a change. I still enjoy cutting wood with my small chain saw.

Another memory I have of those good old days from the 1920's to the 1940's was there were young men who didn't have full time jobs and needed to make money. In the summer when the grain harvest was in the Dakotas you could go out there and get a job in the harvest shocking grain. If you had a little experience with driving horses, they would furnish a team of horses and a wagon to haul grain into the threshing machine or other related jobs. Then, as combines became more popular, this kind of job faded out. Although, if you were willing to work, there was always work to be found during harvest season. There were no unions or minimum wages, so whatever you and the farmer agreed on was it. Grain harvest was from July to September, then in October and November you could go down to Iowa and pick and husk corn before the days of the machine corn pickers.

Then in the winter you could go north to Minnesota and work in the woods, cutting and skidding logs with a two man crosscut saw and horses for skidding, etc. You would stay in a bunkhouse and there would be a cook shack where you would eat. A noon meal was brought out to you in the woods. This era was mostly late 1800's through about the 1930's. There were young people going to college in those days, but the numbers were few compared to now.

Now it is September 21st, 2004, and there have been a lot of happenings since I thought I was almost done in March. This is election year, and I believe this election is probably the most important one since the birth of this great country. This country throughout my lifetime has had two major parties, the Democrats and the Republicans, and some smaller parties that have never been able to get strong enough to have much impact. For most of my years I never really considered whether I was a Democrat or Republican, I just voted for who I thought was the best person for the job. I never considered myself to be a Democrat, and I guess former President Reagan was, but my thinking was much like his. He said "I didn't leave the Democratic party; they left me." The liberal thinking and voting by Democrats has been so much against the thinking of our forefathers. So now I am a Republican, and I am working hard so that this election will come out for the good of our country.

Mr. Carol Peterson
The oldest Peterson left of the Peterson-Okerstrom clan.

Family, 1994.

Carol with great-grandson, Carson.

Irene with one of the many quilts she has made for grandchildren and great-grandchildren.

Carol with grandson, Evan DiMartinis.

Irene's flowers.

Wendy with Reed and Danny.

Four Generation Pictures

L-R: Dwight, Corey, Carol holding Carson.

L-R: Dwight holding Zachary, Carol, Rachel, Alexa.

Back L-R: Susan, Carol, Holly holding Gavyn. Front: Devyn, Payton, Cashton.

Back L-R: Erin, Carol, Arlen holding Austin. Front: Andrea.

L-R: Sarah, Abby, Patty, Irene.

L-R: Susan, Carol, Irene holding Devyn, Holly. Four Generations, 1999.

Carol with Jenna Burton, 2003.

Julie Larson, 1991.

Leah DiMartinis, 1998.

Paige and Isabelle Burton, 2001.

Carol's stepmother Gladys Peterson, 1996.

First family, 1987 at the cemetery.
LrR: Bernice, Arlene, Carol, Pearl, Dorothy.

Irene, Arlene, Dorothy, 1992.

Arlene's children, 1947. L-R: Wayne, Rodney, Sharon.

Dorothy and Harold Baker with Arlene's boys Wayne and Rodney, the little girl with bonnet is their oldest daughter, Darla.

First family, 1994. Back L-R: Pearl, Carol. Front L-R: Dorothy, Arlene, Bernice.

Maple Syrup time.

Carol and Irene, Vacationing

Massachusetts, Mayflower in background.   Florida.

Mark DiMartinis, 1998.

Tammy Burton with Isabelle, 1998.

Allison Peterson, Leah DiMartinis, Paige Burton, Mark DiMartinis, 1998.

Tug-o-war.

Family, 1989.

Spirit Lake, Birchwood Beach on right.

ISBN 1-4120-4622-X

Made in the USA
Lexington, KY
14 December 2010